Student Teacher

Introductory English for Education Majors

Susan Williams
Vivian Morooka

NAN'UN-DO

Student Teacher

Introductory English for Education Majors

Copyright © 2014

Susan Williams
Vivian Morooka

All rights Reserved

No part of this book may be reproduced in any form without written permission from the authors and Nan'un-do Co., Ltd.

Acknowledgement

The authors would like to thank Eiichi Morooka, Hideo Sawaguchi, Terri Sugiura, Ryo Kamiya and Takumi Kamiya for their valuable contributions and assistance. We would also like to thank Kasumi and Andy Sugiura for their help with the art work. In addition we would like to thank the students of Shukutoku University, Department of Welfare of Education and their teacher Paul Entee for their input and feedback during the writing of this book.

Map of the U.S.A. and Canada

Map of the U.K.

Map of Australia

Map of New Zealand

Cursive Writing

Look at the letters below. Practice writing your name a few times on the lines that follow.

A B C D E F G H I J K L M

N O P Q R S T U V W X Y Z

a b c d e f g h i j k l m n o

p q r s t u v w x y z

My name is

Table of Contents

	The Alphabet—Cursive Writing	6
Pre-Unit A	Getting to Know Your Teacher	8
Pre-Unit B	Getting to Know Your Partner	9
Pre-Unit C	Getting to Know Your Group	10
Pre-Unit D	Classroom English	11
Pre-Unit E	Getting to Know One Another	13

Meet the People in This Book   14

Unit 1	Meeting and Greeting	16
Unit 2	Family and Friends	21
Unit 3	Likes and Dislikes	28
Unit 4	Good Habits and Bad Habits	35
Review	Units 1-4	42

Unit 5	Summer and Fun	50
Unit 6	Here and There	56
Unit 7	Giving and Receiving	62
Unit 8	Parties and Fashion	70
Review	Units 5-8	78

Unit 9	Physical Education and Health	86
Unit 10	Nursery School and Day Care	93
Unit 11	Educating and Caring	100
Unit 12	Bullying and Other Problems	108
Review	Units 9-12	113

Pre-Unit A Getting to Know Your Teacher

Your teacher will introduce himself/herself. Listen and then complete the answers to the questions below. Compare your answers with your partner's.

1. What's his/her name?

    His/Her name is _____.

2. Where does he/she come from? (What city, state, country?)

    He/She comes from _____.

3. Where does he/she live now?

    He/She lives in _____.

4. How many people are there in his/her family? Who are they?

    There are _____ people in his/her family.

    They are his/her _____.

5. How long has he/she been in Japan?

    He/She has been in Japan for _____ years.

6. How long has he/she been teaching English?

    He/She has been teaching English for _____ years.

7. What does he/she like to do in his/her free time?

    He/She likes to _____.

8. Who's his/her favorite singer or group?

    It's _____.

9. What special talent does he/she have?

    He/She can _____.

10. When's his/her birthday?

    His/Her birthday is on _____.

Pre-Unit B Getting to Know Your Partner

Take turns asking and answering the questions below with your partner. Answer in full sentences. Write your partner's answers on the lines. Write exactly what he/she says. Begin with "I/My ..."

1. What's your name?
   " _____ "

2. Where are you from?
   " _____ "

3. Where do you live now?
   " _____ "

4. How many brothers and sisters do you have?
   " _____ "

5. Are they older or younger?
   " _____ "

6. Which high school did you graduate from?
   " _____ "

7. What do you like to do in your free time?
   " _____ "

8. Who's your favorite singer?
   " _____ "

9. When's your birthday?
   " _____ "

10. What special talent do you have?
    " _____ "

11. Why do you want to be a teacher?
    " _____ "

Pre-Unit C   Getting to Know Your Group

Get together with another pair. Introduce your partner to them. Use his/her answers from Pre-Unit B and these sentence patterns. Then listen to the other pair as they introduce each other. Make notes in the boxes below.

1. This is ...
2. He/She's from ...
3. He/She lives in ...
4. He/She has ... (older/younger) brothers and/or (older/younger) sisters.
   He/She is an only child.
5. He/She graduated from ... High School.
6. He/She likes to ... in his/her free time.
7. His/her favorite singer is ...
8. His/Her birthday is on ...
9. He/She is special because he/she can ...
10. He/She wants to be a teacher because ...

MY GROUP

	Name, Hometown, Live now	Family (brothers and sisters)	High School	Interests (free time)	Favorite singer	Birthday, Special feature	Why a teacher?
Me							
My partner							
Other pair (1)							
Other pair (2)							

Pre-Unit D   Classroom English

Here are some things your TEACHER may say to you: 02

1. Open your books to page 13.
2. Close your books.
3. Please repeat./Repeat after me.
4. Clear your desks. (for a game, test, etc.)
5. Raise your hand./Put up your hand.
6. Pass your papers to the front.
7. Pass these papers around. (back)
8. Take out paper and a pencil.
9. Do Exercise 1 for homework. (now with your partner)
10. Work in pairs. (with a partner) (in groups)
11. Cover your textbook./Cover the conversation.
12. Do you understand? (Answer: Yes, I do./ No, I don't.)
13. Check your answers with your partner.
14. Exchange papers.

Here are some things YOU may need to say to your teacher.   03

1. I have a question.
2. What does this mean? (that) (vocational school, major, etc.)
3. Say that again, please. / Please repeat that. / Pardon me?
4. May I go to the restroom? (lavatory) / May I be excused, please?
5. I'm not feeling well. May I leave?
6. I'm sorry I was late. The train was late. (I overslept.)
7. I'm sorry I was absent last week. I had a cold. (the flu)
8. I'm going to be absent next week. I have a doctor's (dental) appointment.
9. Can I have the handouts (copies) from last week?
10. How do you say (pronounce) this?
11. How do you spell that (international, library, etc.)?
12. I don't understand this (that).
13. How do you say natto in English?
14. What do you call this (that) in English?
15. These handouts (copies) are extras.
16. There aren't enough handouts (copies).
17. What does "USA" stand for? (Answer: It stands for the "United States of America".)

Here are some things YOU and YOUR PARTNER may need to say to each other. 04

1. Let's practice together.
2. You go first.
3. I'll go first.
4. I'll be "A", and you be "B."
5. It's <u>my</u> (<u>your</u>) (<u>his</u>) (<u>her</u>) turn.
6. Is it my turn?
7. It's not your turn.
8. My partner is absent. Can I practice with you?
9. I forgot my textbook. Can I share your book?
10. Can I borrow your <u>eraser</u> (<u>pencil</u>)?

Practice writing your signature here. Use the letters on the Cursive Writing page as a model.

Pre-Unit E Getting To Know One Another

Walk around the room and ask your teacher and your classmates the questions below. When someone answers "Yes," ask him or her to sign on the line. The same person can only sign ONE time.

Practice these question patterns with your partner before you start.

| Are you | an only child? on a diet? | Yes, I am. No, I'm not. | Can you | play tennis? ski? | Yes, I can. No, I can't. |
| Do you | like natto? have a sister? | Yes, I do. No, I don't. | Were you | born in the summer? at home yesterday? | Yes, I was. No, I wasn't. |

Look for a classmate who …

(Make sure you use the correct verb form when you ask the question.)*

1. … is an only child.
   (Are you …?)

2. … was born in the summer
   (Were you …?)

3. … likes spaghetti
   (Do you …?)

4. … can ski.
   (Can you …?)

5. … gets up early.
   (Do you …?)

6. … can play the piano.
   (Can you play …?)

7. … likes to study.
   (Do you …?)

8. … is on a diet.
   (Are you …?)

9. …has two brothers.
   (Do you have …?)

10. … likes rock music.
    (Do you …?)

11. … comes from a big city.
    (Do you …?)

12. … has a dog.
    (Do you …?)

13. … is a good swimmer.
    (Are you …?)

14. … likes English.
    (Do you …?)

15. … is hungry.
    (Are you …?)

* He/She/a classmate like<u>s</u> …
   You like …

Meet the People in This Book

These are some of the people you'll meet in this book:

Erika Kaneko

 05

Erika is 18 years old. She's a university student. She lives in Sakura, Chiba. She wants to be a pre-school teacher. Next summer holiday, Erika plans to visit the United States. She wants to see New York. She plans to go with her best friend, Yurika. There are four people in Erika's family: her mother, her father, her older brother Aki, and Erika. Erika and Yurika belong to the English Conversation Club. They want to practice speaking English to get ready for their holiday in the United States. Erika likes animals. She has a cat called "Lucky."

Takumi Yamaguchi

 06

Takumi is 19 years old. He's from Nagano. He wants to work at a school for children with special needs. He doesn't want to teach in a classroom, though. He wants to look after the children who live in the dormitory. In his free time, he likes to play games on his computer. Sometimes he goes to Akihabara with his friend, Koji, to look at computers. He wants to study in the U.K. next year. Takumi has an older brother and a younger sister. They live at home with their mother. She is British. They have two dogs, Benny and Baron. Benny is a Labrador and Baron is a Shiba.

Yusuke Takada

Yusuke is 20 years old. He's a freshman at a university. He's from Saitama. He wants to be a health and physical education teacher. He likes sports and martial arts. His favorite sport is baseball. At his university, he belongs to the Japanese archery club. Yusuke lives with his mother and father in Tokyo now. He is an only child. In his free time, he likes to go to the movies or to Disneyland with his girlfriend. He likes animals, but he doesn't have any pets because he and his parents live in a condominium.

Mr. James W. Wilson

Mr. Wilson is 40 years old. He's from Sydney, Australia. He's the instructor for the first-year English Conversation Course. Mr. Wilson likes to travel. Every summer he and his family go to a different country for two weeks. Last year they went to Egypt. Next summer they want to go to Finland. In their free time, they like to grow organic vegetables in their garden. They have so many vegetables that they give most of them to their friends and neighbors. In return, the neighbors look after the Wilsons' cats when they go on vacation.

Unit 1   Meeting and Greeting

I. Warm-Up:

A. Finish the short conversations below by matching the questions/comments on the left with the responses on the right. Work with a partner.

_d_ 1. Hi, I'm Terry Freeman.   a. It's Education.
____ 2. Hello, Catherine.   b. Please call me Cathy.
____ 3. What's your major?   c. Nice to meet you too, Erika.
____ 4. Nice to meet you, Carlos.   d. Hi, Terry, I'm Cindy Lee.
____ 5. How do you do?   e. No, I'm from Australia.
____ 6. Good to meet you, Jane.   f. Yes, I do. I live on campus.
____ 7. Where are you from, Carlos?   g. Good morning, Mr. Wilson.
____ 8. Do you live near the university?   h. How do you do?
____ 9. Are you from New Zealand?   i. I'm from Brazil.
____ 10. Good morning, John.   j. Good to meet you, too.

B. Now practice the short conversations with your partner.

II. Vocabulary:

The university subjects below are hidden in the box. Find and circle each subject. The words can be horizontal, vertical, or diagonal. Work with a partner.

> nursing   education   pre-school (education)   medicine   history
> literature   health   physical (education)   special (education)   English

S	P	E	C	I	A	L	N	E	E	D	H
F	D	D	Z	M	E	D	I	C	I	N	E
L	N	U	X	S	O	M	B	U	Q	R	X
I	U	C	C	H	E	N	G	L	I	S	H
T	R	A	X	P	E	R	K	A	L	I	I
E	S	T	O	I	H	A	E	M	P	B	S
R	I	I	Z	C	O	Y	L	N	S	O	T
A	N	O	K	T	Z	S	S	T	Y	E	O
T	G	N	E	Q	P	G	I	I	H	K	R
U	U	M	M	Q	O	S	U	M	C	O	Y
R	P	Z	O	G	L	K	U	R	J	A	A
E	S	P	R	E	-	S	C	H	O	O	L

† Look up new vocabulary in your dictionary.

III. Dialogue:

A. Today, Professor Wilson and his students are meeting one another for the first time. As you listen to the conversation below, fill in the blanks.   09

Mr. Wilson: (1) _____ _____, everyone. I'm Jim Wilson, and I'm your teacher for this first-year (2) _____ _____ course. Please call me Mr. Wilson.

Students: Good morning, Mr. Wilson.

Mr. Wilson: I'm from (3) _____, Australia, but I (4) _____ in Chiba now. Please introduce yourselves. Let's start with you.

Erika: (5) _____ _____ _____ _____, everybody? I'm Erika, Erika Kaneko, and I live in Sakura. My major is (6) _____ Education.

Mr. Wilson: Thank you Erika. Who's next?

Takumi: (7) _____ _____. My name's Takumi Yamaguchi. I live near the university now, but I'm from Nagano. My major is (8) _____ Education.

Mr. Wilson: Thank you, Takumi. Who's next?

Yusuke: Me. I'm Yusuke Takada and (9) _____ _____ _____ Saitama, but I live in Tokyo now. My major is (10) _____ and Physical Education.

Mr. Wilson: Thank you, Yusuke.

(After all the students have finished introducing themselves:)

Mr. Wilson: Let's take a short break now. I will tell you all about this course when you come back. See you in ten minutes. Don't be late!

B. Now make groups of four people. Practice the dialogue four times, changing roles each time.

Unit 1   Meeting and Greeting   17

IV. Check Your Understanding:

Work with a partner. Take turns asking and answering these questions about the dialogue. Write the answers on the lines in full sentences.

1. What does Mr. Wilson teach? _____
2. Where does Mr. Wilson come from? _____
3. What's Erika's major? _____
4. Where does Takumi live? _____
5. Where's Yusuke from? _____
6. What's Yusuke's major? _____

V. Conversation Check:

A. Tell your partner about yourself. If you are not sure what to say, use the pattern below.

I'm _____. I live in _____. My major is _____.

If you live in Chiba now (for example) but you lived somewhere else before, don't forget to say: "I live in Chiba now, but I come from ___(Shizuoka)___."

B. Now your teacher will ask some students to introduce themselves to the class.

VI. Asking for More Information:

Do you remember how to ask about birthdays and other personal information? Fill in the blanks with a question word and then ask and answer the questions with your partner.

Partner's answers

1. _____ old are you? _____
2. _____ is your birthday? _____
3. _____ is your blood type? _____
4. _____ do you live? _____
5. _____ are you from? _____

VII. Grammar Check:

A. Compare the verb forms in these questions and answers.

Where *are* you from?   I*'m* from Korea.

Where *do* you *live*?   I *live* in Japan.

Where *does* Mr. Wilson *live*?   He *lives* in Tokyo.

B. Fill in each blank with the correct form of a verb.

1. You _____ a professor.

2. What _____ your blood type?

3. Where _____ you from?

4. Where _____ Takumi live?

5. What _____ Erika's major?

VIII. Look At This:

A. Here are some university departments and subjects. Repeat them after your teacher.

Education	Social Sciences	Liberal Arts
Special Education	Sociology	English Literature
Pre-school Education	Social Welfare	Foreign Languages
Primary/Elementary Education	Anthropology	History
Secondary Education	Political Science	Art
Health and Physical Education	Philosophy	Economics

B. Look up the departments/subjects you don't know in a dictionary. Work with a partner. Then write down the names of some other subjects you know.

_____

_____

_____

_____

IX. Conversation Practice:

Use what you have learned in this unit to complete the dialogue below. Work with a partner. First, practice the dialogue as Takumi and Erika. Then practice it using your own names and majors.

Student A: Hello, I'm Takumi. _____.

Student B: _____, Takumi. I'm Erika.

Student A: Are you from Chiba?

Student B: _____. Where are you from?

Student A: I'm from _____.

Student B: Are you in the _____ Department?

Student A: _____. My major is _____. What about you?

Student B: My major is _____.

Student A: Great! It's lunchtime, Erika. Shall we have lunch together?

Student B: Yes, let's.

Unit 2   Family and Friends

I.   Warm-up:

A. Finish the short conversations below by matching the questions on the left with the responses on the right. Work with a partner.

_____	1. What's your telephone number?	a.	I'm a student.
_____	2. Could you help me?	b.	It's 090-1234-5679.
_____	3. What do you do?	c.	I'm listening to the teacher.
_____	4. How are you doing?	d.	It's December 21, 1991.
_____	5. What are you doing?	e.	Fine, thanks, and you?
_____	6. When's your birthday?	f.	He's a businessman.
_____	7. What's your date of birth?	g.	It's 285-1104.
_____	8. What does your father do?	h.	Sure. What can I do for you?
_____	9. What's your postal code?	i.	It's 310 Nakadai, Narita.
_____	10. What's your address?	j.	It's August fifth.

B. Now practice the short conversations with your partner.

II.   Vocabulary:

Fill in the blank in each sentence below with the correct form of one of the words/phrases in this box. Work with a partner.

> fill out   application form   middle names   postal code   housewife
> ward   prefecture   date of birth   full name   younger   young

1. My mother is a _____. Her main job is to take care of our family and house.
2. In Japan, most people don't have _____.
3. Toru's sister is only three years old. She is very _____.
4. When I put my name, address, and telephone number on a form, I _____ the form.
5. Japan has 43 _____, called "ken" in Japanese.
6. My _____ brother wants to get a job, so he has to fill out an _____ with a company.
7. Your _____ is your first name, your last name, and, if you have one, your middle name.
8. John's _____ is January 22, 1988.
9. Their address is 13-23-608 Asahi, Wakaba-_____, Chiba.
10. Our _____ is part of our address.

III. Dialogue:

A. Takumi is in the cafeteria with a friend. He sees Mr. Wilson. As you listen to their conversation, fill in the blanks. 🔵 10

Takumi: Hello, Mr. Wilson.

Mr. Wilson: Hello. (1) _____ _____ _____ _____?

Takumi: Great! Mr. Wilson, could you help me (2) _____ _____ this application form? I want to study in the U.K. next year.

Mr. Wilson: Sure. May I see it? I can fill it out for you. OK, what's your last name?

Takumi: It's Yamaguchi.

Mr. Wilson: And your first name's Takeshi?

Takumi: No, it isn't. It's Takumi, but I don't know what to write here. I don't have a (3) _____ _____.

Mr. Wilson: Then you don't need to write anything there. And what's your (4) _____ _____ _____?

Takumi: I (5) _____ _____ _____ February 29th, 1992.

Mr. Wilson: Oh, that's unusual. There aren't many people born on February 29th. Next question: what job do you have? I mean, (6) _____ _____ _____ _____?

Takumi: I'm a student, but I work at a restaurant, too, so I'm also (7) _____ _____.

Mr. Wilson: OK, and what's your address?

Takumi: It's 180 Daiganji, Apartment 419, (8) _____, Chiba-city.

Mr. Wilson: That's in Chiba Prefecture, right? And what's your (9) _____ _____?

Takumi: It's 286-1701.

Mr. Wilson: What's your telephone number?

Takumi: It's (10) _____.

Mr. Wilson: You're finished! Just sign your name here.

Takumi: Thank you very much, Mr. Wilson.

Mr. Wilson: You're welcome. Anytime you need help, just ask.

B. Practice the dialogue twice with a partner, changing roles each time.

IV. Check Your Understanding:

Work with a partner. Take turns asking and answering these questions about the dialogue. Write the answers on the lines in full sentences.

1. What's Mr. Yamaguchi's first name?

   _____

2. Why does he want to fill out an application form?

   _____

3. Why can't he write his middle name?

   _____

4. What does he do?

   _____

5. What's his address?

   _____

6. When was he born?

   _____

V. Conversation Check:

Tell your partner your first name, your last name, your date of birth, and what your parents do. If you are not sure what to say, use the patterns below.

My first name is ….
My last name is ….
My date of birth is ….*
There are _____ people in my family.**
My father is a ….
My mother is a ….

(*Your date of birth is the MONTH, DAY, and YEAR you were born. **Don't forget to include yourself!)

Unit 2 Family and Friends   23

VI. Asking for More Information:

A. Write the questions you need to ask to get the following information. Work with a partner.

1. full name: _____?
2. address: _____?
3. telephone number: _____?
4. postal code: _____?
5. job: _____?
6. father's job: _____?
7. mother's job: _____?
8. date of birth: _____?
9. number of people in your family: _____?
10. brothers/sisters: _____?

B. Now ask your partner the questions in "A." Write your partner's answers here.

1. "_____."
2. "_____."
3. "_____."
4. "_____."
5. "_____."
6. "_____."
7. "_____."
8. "_____."
9. "_____."
10. "_____."

VII. Grammar Check:

Write the negative form of each sentence below. Follow the example. Work with a partner.

Example:

My name is John.   *My name isn't John. / My name's not John.*

1. I have a middle name.
2. My date of birth is January 1, 1991.
3. John has a brother.
4. I'm fine.
5. I have a part-time job.
6. My father is a civil servant.
7. We are Special Education majors.
8. Charles lives at 12-22-101 Nakadai, Bunkyo-ku, Tokyo.
9. Susan can play the piano.
10. My mother works in a library.

VIII. Look At This:

This is an application form for a part-time job. Work with a partner. Fill out the form with your partner's information. Ask him/her the questions you need to get the information.

<table>
<tr><td colspan="4" align="center">APPLICATION FORM
Today's Date:</td></tr>
<tr><td rowspan="2">NAME</td><td align="center">Last</td><td align="center">First</td><td align="center">Middle</td></tr>
<tr><td></td><td></td><td></td></tr>
<tr><td>SEX (circle)</td><td colspan="3" align="center">Male   Female</td></tr>
<tr><td rowspan="2">DATE OF BIRTH</td><td align="center">Month</td><td align="center">Day</td><td align="center">Year</td></tr>
<tr><td></td><td></td><td></td></tr>
<tr><td>ADDRESS</td><td colspan="3"></td></tr>
<tr><td>POSTAL CODE</td><td colspan="3"></td></tr>
<tr><td>TELEPHONE NUMBER</td><td colspan="3"></td></tr>
<tr><td>FATHER'S/MOTHER'S JOB(s)</td><td colspan="3"></td></tr>
<tr><td>WHAT DO YOU DO?</td><td colspan="3"></td></tr>
</table>

IX. Conversation Practice:

Use what you have learned in this unit to complete the dialogue below. Work with a partner. Practice the dialogue twice, first as Student A, then as Student B. Write your partner's answers on the lines.

Student A: Could you please help me fill out this form?

Student B: _____. What's your first name?

Student A: It's _____.

Student B: What's your last name?

Student A: It's _____.

Student B: What's your middle name?

Student A: _____.

Student B: What's your date of birth?

Student A: It's _____.

Student B: What do you do?

Student A: _____.

Student B: What's your address?

Student A: It's _____.

Student B: What's your postal code?

Student A: It's _____.

Student B: And your telephone number?

Student A: It's _____.

Student B: How many people are there in your family?

Student A: There are _____ people in my family: my _____ and me.

Student B: What does your father do?

Student A: He _____.

Student B: And your mother?

Student A: She _____.

Student B: OK, you're finished. Please sign here.

Student A: _____.

Student B: _____.

Unit 3 Likes and Dislikes

I. Warm-Up:

A. Finish the short conversations below by matching the questions on the left with the answers on the right. Work with a partner.

____ 1. Do you like Chinese food?   a. I like mystery stories.
____ 2. Does he like golf?   b. Yes. They are exciting!
____ 3. What do you think of the "Harry Potter" movies?   c. No, they prefer to play tennis.
____ 4. Do Yusuke and Erika like rock music?   d. She likes Italian food best.
____ 5. Does she like reading?   e. I like listening to music.
____ 6. What's your hobby?   f. Yes. She likes romance novels.
____ 7. What's your favorite kind of book?   g. Yes, he does.
____ 8. Do you like action movies?   h. Yes, they do. They think it's cool.
____ 9. Do they like to play soccer?   i. They're terrific!
____ 10. What's Erika's favorite kind of food?   j. Yes, I love it!

B. Now practice the short conversations with your partner.

II. Vocabulary:

A. List the words/phrases in this box under the correct categories.

> Chinese   romance   rock   reading   French   listening to music
> J-pop   action   mystery   Italian   playing computer games
> horror   heavy metal   classical   bowling   Japanese

Food	Movies	Hobbies	Music
_____	_____	_____	_____
_____	_____	_____	_____
_____	_____	_____	_____
_____	_____	_____	_____

B. Here are some more words that you will use in this unit. Write the Japanese meaning for each word. (If you don't know what a word means, look it up in your dictionary.) Then write an example of something that each word could describe. Follow this example. Don't use the same example twice. Work with a partner.

Example:　　great　　すばらしい　　　　　　　a great movie

1. exciting　　　　_____　　_____

2. terrific　　　　_____　　_____

3. cool　　　　　 _____　　_____

4. cute　　　　　 _____　　_____

5. boring　　　　 _____　　_____

6. terrible　　　　_____　　_____

7. horrible　　　　_____　　_____

8. wonderful　　　_____　　_____

9. awesome　　　 _____　　_____

10. awful　　　　 _____　　_____

Unit 3　Likes and Dislikes　29

III. Dialogue:

A. Erika is studying at a coffee shop near the university. Yusuke sees her as he is walking by. He goes in to talk to her. As you listen to their conversation, fill in the blanks.

Yusuke: Hi Erika! How's it going?

Erika: (1) _____! I mean, I've been really busy, but it is so exciting to be in college. I love it!

Yusuke: That's great! Oh, Erika, do you mind if I talk to you for a few (2) _____?

Erika: Not at all. Have a seat.

Yusuke: I want to ask your advice about a (3) _____ present for my girlfriend, Megumi.

Erika: Well, what does she like to do? Does she like to read? Does she like (4) _____? What sports does she like to play?

Yusuke: Hmm. I don't think she likes to read that much. She loves (5) _____ movies, and she likes to play tennis and swim.

Erika: Well, how about getting her a DVD of the latest Johnny Depp movie? I heard it's (6) _____. Or you could get her a (7) _____ bag to carry her stuff in. They have some at the mall, and they're on sale now. They're really (8) _____.

Yusuke: Great idea. She'd probably like that. Thanks a lot, Erika. I really needed your help! Last year I didn't give her anything. She didn't speak to me for a (9) _____!

Erika: How (10) _____! You really do need help!

B. Practice the dialogue twice with a partner, changing roles each time.

IV. Check Your Understanding:

Work with a partner. Take turns asking and answering these questions about the dialogue. Write the answers on the lines in full sentences.

1. Why does Yusuke want to talk to Erika?
   _____

2. Does Megumi like to read?
   _____

3. What kind of movies does Megumi like?
   _____

4. What is on sale at the mall now?
   _____

5. What present did Yusuke give his girlfriend last year?
   _____

V. Conversation Check:

A. Look at the examples in this box. Next, complete the questions below with words from Part II, A and B. Then answer the questions with your own likes and dislikes.

Do you like Chinese food?	Yes, I think it's great! / No, I like Italian.
What's your favorite kind of movie?	I like action movies best. I think they're exciting.
What's your hobby?	My hobby is playing computer games.

1. Do you like _____? _____ I think it's/they're _____

2. What's your favorite _____? I like _____ best.
   I think it's/they're _____.

3. What's your hobby? _____

B. With a partner, practice asking and answering each other's questions.

Unit 3   Likes and Dislikes   31

VI. Asking for More Information:

A. Get together in a group. Use the patterns in Part V to ask each other questions. Write each person's answers in the appropriate boxes.

Partners' Names				
Food _____ (Write a kind of food: for example, "Italian")				
Movie				
Music				
Hobby				

B. The teacher will choose some students to talk about another student in their group. When it's your turn, use sentences like this:

He/She likes/doesn't like _____.

His/Her favorite _____ is _____.

His/Her hobby is _____.

VII. Grammar Check:

A. Read through these sentences with your teacher.

I/We/They like to	read.	I/We/They want to	travel to Egypt.
We/They	play computer games.		win the lottery.
He/She likes to	sew.	He/She wants to	go snowboarding.

I/We/They prefer to	study in the library.	My/Our/Their favorite singer is Taylor Swift.
	eat organic vegetables.	
He/She prefers to	wake up early.	His/Her favorite Movie is "Princess Mononoke."

B. Complete these sentences with real information about yourself and the following people. Make sure you use the correct verb forms.

1. I like to _____
2. My friend (like) _____
3. I prefer to _____
4. My mother (prefer) _____
5. I want to _____
6. My friends (want) _____
7. My favorite movie is _____
8. My mother/father's (favorite) _____

VIII. Look At This:

A. This is a list of some of the most popular things in the world:

Books	1. The Bible (over six billion copies printed as of 2014)
	2. "Harry Potter Series" by J.K.Rowling (more than 450 million copies sold as of 2014)
Movies	1. "Avatar" (made more than $2.7 billion as of 2014)
	2. "Titanic" is the second most popular. It made more than $1.9 billion before it was released in a 3D version in 2012.
Song	1. "White Christmas" by Bing Crosby (more than 50 million copies sold)
	2. "Candle in the Wind 1997" by Elton John (a tribute to the late Diana, Princess of Wales, sold 33 million copies)
Food	1. Pasta 2. Meat 3. Rice

B. What do you think the most popular things in Japan are? Work with your group.

1. Books: _____
2. Movies: _____
3. Songs: _____
4. Food: _____

Unit 3   Likes and Dislikes   33

IX. Conversation Practice:

Use what you have learned in this unit to complete the dialogue below. Answer with real information. Practice the dialogue twice, first as Student A, then as Student B. Write your partner's answers on the lines.

Student A is doing a survey of his classmates.

Student A: May I ask you some questions?

Student B: Sure.

Student A: Do you like _____?

Student B: _____. I think it's/they're _____.

Student A: What's your favorite kind of _____?

Student B: My favorite kind of _____ is _____.

Student A: Why?

Student B: I think it's/they're _____.

Student A: Do you like to study in the library or in your room?

Student B: I prefer to study _____.

Student A: What do you like to do in your free time?

Student B: I like to _____.

Student A: What's your hobby?

Student B: My hobby is _____.

Student A: What do you want to do this weekend?

Student B: I want to _____.

Student A: OK. Thank you very much for your time.

Student B: You're welcome.

Unit 4   Good Habits and Bad Habits

I. Warm-up:

A. Finish the short conversations below by matching the questions on the left with the answers on the right. Work with a partner.

____ 1. Do you get enough sleep?   a. No, I really hate the smell of it.
____ 2. Do you eat a lot of fatty food?   b. Yes. I walk more than 10,000 steps a day.
____ 3. How often do you exercise?   c. Yes, it's very relaxing.
____ 4. Do you walk every day?   d. I swim in the pool once a week.
____ 5. Do you go to aerobics classes?   e. About seven hours.
____ 6. How long did you sleep last night?   f. Yes. I love fried chicken.
____ 7. Do you take any medicine?   g. Yes. I like to go hiking.
____ 8. Do you do yoga?   h. Yes. I belong to a sports club.
____ 9. Do you spend a lot of time outdoors?   i. No. I usually go to bed late.
____ 10. Do you smoke?   j. Only when I'm really sick.

B. Now practice the short conversations with your partner.

II. Vocabulary:

These "health" words are hidden in the box. Find and circle each word. The words can be horizontal, vertical or diagonal. Work with a partner.

> exercise   yoga   meditate   vegetables   smoke   vitamins
> junk food   carbohydrate   relax   outdoors   fat   sleep

C	J	O	V	E	X	E	R	C	I	S	E
A	U	T	O	I	R	K	U	K	Q	L	R
R	N	X	F	A	T	K	W	M	W	E	J
B	K	O	P	Z	O	A	H	E	Y	E	I
O	W	U	F	E	Y	P	M	D	U	P	U
H	F	T	X	S	F	O	E	I	D	B	T
Y	O	D	H	B	M	M	G	T	N	P	M
D	O	O	P	V	Q	O	A	A	K	S	O
R	D	O	E	O	U	F	K	T	A	H	R
A	Q	R	K	T	H	K	R	E	L	A	X
T	U	S	L	L	S	E	G	Z	P	G	I
E	A	V	E	G	E	T	A	B	L	E	S

III. Dialogue:

A. Classes are over for the day, and Takumi and Yusuke are waiting for the bus to take them to the train station. As you listen to their conversation, fill in the blanks.

Yusuke: Hi, Takumi. When does this bus leave?

Takumi: It leaves at (1) _____. It's nearly five o'clock now. Are you in a hurry?

Yusuke: Yes. My (2) _____ class at the gym starts at 5:30. I don't want to be late.

Takumi: Don't worry! You'll be (3) _____ _____. How often do you go to the gym?

Yusuke: I usually go twice a week, on Mondays and Wednesdays. I don't get enough (4) _____ at school to keep fit.

Takumi: I don't really like exercise. I'm a real "couch potato." I like to watch TV and play computer games. What else do you do?

Yusuke: Well, I really try to stay healthy, so I exercise, and I don't eat (5) _____ _____ or drink soda.

Takumi: That's impressive! I don't (6) _____, but I eat a lot of (7) _____ _____ now that I live alone. It's so easy!

Yusuke: I know what you mean, but it's really (8) _____ _____ _____. It's difficult to get enough sleep, too. Do you have a part-time job?

Takumi: Yes. I work the late shift (9) _____ _____ a week, so I never get enough sleep. I start work at nine o'clock tonight.

Yusuke: Well, don't work too hard. And (10) _____ _____ _____ for class tomorrow morning!

Takumi: Right. I'll do my best. Have a good time at the gym!

B. Practice the dialogue twice with a partner, changing roles each time.

IV. Check Your Understanding:

Work with a partner. Take turns asking and answering these questions about the dialogue. Write the answers on the lines in full sentences.

1. How often does Yusuke go to the gym?
   _____

2. What else does Yusuke do to stay healthy?
   _____

3. What does Takumi like to do in his free time?
   _____

4. How many times a week does Takumi work at his part-time job?
   _____

5. What time does Takumi start work tonight?
   _____

6. Do Takumi and Yusuke smoke?
   _____

V. Conversation Check:

Using the examples below, ask your partner about his/her lifestyle. Think of three more examples. Write your partner's answers on the lines.

Do you ...?

1. ... drink a lot of soda? _____
2. ... get enough sleep? _____
3. ... go to a sports club? _____
4. ... eat enough vegetables? _____
5. ... go to bed late? _____
6. ... play a lot of computer games? _____
7. ... _____ ? _____
8. ... _____ ? _____
9. ... _____ ? _____

Unit 4   Good Habits and Bad Habits

VI. Asking for More Information:

Now work in a group and use the conversation patterns below to ask and answer questions about each other's lifestyles. Use the questions from Part V.

Student A:	Do you get enough sleep?
Student B:	Yes, I do. I get seven hours of sleep every night.
Student A:	Do you eat a lot of fruit and vegetables?
Student B:	No, I don't. I only eat bananas, and I hate vegetables.

VII. Grammar Check:

A: Look at the table below. Repeat the short conversations in the table after your teacher. Then practice them with members of your group.

How often	do	you	spend time outdoors?	Once a day.
			eat fast food?	Twice a week.
	does	Yusuke	exercise?	Every day.
		Takumi	drink soda?	Almost never.
		(a member of your group)	do sports?	Never.

B: Now unscramble each question below. Write the questions on the first line. Check your answers with the teacher, and then ask a partner each question. Write his/her answers on the second line.

1. you / fruit / like / vegetables / and / to / a / lot / do / eat / of

   _____?
   _____.

2. day / does / mother / exercise / your / every

   _____?
   _____.

3. a / you / do / go / three / gym / the / to / week / times

   _____?
   _____.

4. junk / food / eat / how / do / often / you

   _____?
   _____.

5. often / Internet / how / do / games / play / on / you / the

   _____?
   _____.

VIII. Look At This:

A. **Telling Time:**
There are two main ways to tell the time in English. One way is to say the hour first. You probably know this way. The second way is to say the minutes first. This is the more natural way to tell the time in daily conversation. Practice saying these times with your teacher.

Hours first	Minutes first
1:05 = one oh five	five past one / five after one
1:10 = one ten	ten past one / ten after one
1:15 = one fifteen	a quarter past one / a quarter after one
1:30 = one thirty	half past one
1:35 = one thirty-five	twenty-five to two
1:45 = one forty-five	a quarter to two

Special Note (1):

- When someone asks you "What's the time?" or "What time is it?" you should answer;

    "It's ten past four." OR "It's a quarter to five."

- When someone asks you the time that something happens—for example, "What time do you have dinner?" or "What time does the first lesson start?" —you should answer using "at": "I have dinner <u>at</u> half past seven." OR "The first lesson starts <u>at</u> nine o'clock."

B. Draw hands on these clocks to show different times. When you have finished, show your partner and ask "What time is it?" for each clock. When your partner answers, write the times in words on the lines below.

1. It's _____.

2. _____.

3. _____.

4. _____.

Unit 4 Good Habits and Bad Habits

C. Now ask your partner about these opening and closing and beginning and ending times.

1.

You:	What time does the bank open?
Partner:	_____ .
You:	What time does it close?
Partner:	_____ .

2.

You:	What time does the movie begin?
Partner:	_____ .
You:	What time does it end?
Partner:	_____ .

Special Note (2):

- In everyday conversation you don't need to give exact times such as 9:58 or 3:41. Instead, you can give the approximate time using "about," "almost," "a little after," or "just after."
  Look at these examples:

  3:21 = It's a little after twenty past three. 12:29 = It's almost half past twelve.
  8:01 = It's about eight o'clock. 5:47 = It's just after a quarter to six.

- In the U.K., you can also say "nearly half past twelve" (12:29) or "just gone twenty past three" (3:21).

- When you don't need to give an exact time for something (meeting someone at a restaurant, for example), you can use "ish": "Let's meet at eight-ish." (=about 8:00)

- Of course, when someone needs to know the exact time (of a bus, train, etc.), you can use the "hours first" form, as in:

"The next train is at one thirty-three." (1:33) "You should take the five twenty-six (5:26) bus."

IX. Conversation Practice:

Use what you have learned in this unit to complete the dialogue below. With a partner, practice the dialogue twice, first as Student A, then as Student B.

Student A: What time does your last class finish today, _____?

Student B: It finishes _____. Why?

Student A: I'm going to the supermarket. Do you want to come with me?

Student B: Sure. I need to go shopping, too. What time shall we meet?

Student A: Let's meet _____.

We can get the bus _____.

Student B: OK. What are you going to buy?

Student A: I need to buy some _____.

What about you?

Student B: Just _____.

Student A: _____! Junk food is _____!

You really need to be more careful about your diet.

Student B: But I love it. It's _____.

Unit 4   Good Habits and Bad Habits   41

Review Units 1 – 4

I. Unit 1   Meeting and Greeting

A. Write full questions based on the hints below. Work with a partner.

1. How ... do? (first greeting) _____
2. name? _____
3. from Tokyo? _____
4. from? _____
5. birthday? _____
6. live near the university? _____
7. live? _____
8. your best friend live? _____
9. old? _____
10. major? _____

B. Ask your partner the questions above and write your partner's answers on the lines. When your partner asks you the questions, answer about yourself.

1. "_____"
2. "_____"
3. "_____"
4. "_____"
5. "_____"
6. "_____"
7. "_____"
8. "_____"
9. "_____"
10. "_____"

C. Work with a partner. Write all the names in English of the Education, Social Sciences, and Liberal Arts university majors that you and your partner can think of.

Education	Social Sciences	Liberal Arts
_____	_____	_____
_____	_____	_____
_____	_____	_____
_____	_____	_____
_____	_____	_____

II. Unit 2   Family and Friends

A. Write the questions you need to get the information for an application form. Work with a partner.

1. first name: _____?
2. middle name: _____?
3. last name: _____?
4. job: _____?
5. address: _____?
6. postal code: _____?
7. date of birth: _____?
8. telephone number: _____?
9. father's job: _____?
10. mother's job: _____?

B. Ask your partner the questions above and fill out this form with his/her information.

APPLICATION FORM		Today's Date:	
NAME	Last name	First Name	Middle Name
DATE OF BIRTH	Month	Day	Year
ADDRESS			
Postal Code			
TELEPHONE NUMBER			
Job			
Father's Job			
Mother's Job			

C. Write the negative form of each sentence. Work with a partner. Use contractions.

1. I swim every day.
2. I'm 21 years old.
3. My brother works at a nursery school.
4. Sally is married.
5. Nancy's aunt can sew well.
6. We are all good at math.
7. His sister lives in Tokyo.
8. I have a middle name.
9. You go bowling on weekends.
10. It's raining outside.

III. Unit 3   Likes and Dislikes

A. Ask your partner the following questions. Write down his/her answers in full sentences.

1. What's your hobby? "_____"
2. What's your favorite food? "_____"
3. Do you like to read? "_____"
4. What's your favorite kind of movie? "_____"
5. What TV show do you like? "_____"
6. What do you like to do in the evening? "_____"
7. Who's your favorite singer or group? "_____"
8. What do you think about the latest phones? "_____"
9. What's your favorite sport? "_____"
10. What kind of music do you like? "_____"

B. Work with a partner. Make up and write a sentence using each of these words.

1. exciting _____
2. terrific _____
3. cute _____
4. cool _____
5. boring _____
6. horrible _____
7. awful _____
8. wonderful _____
9. terrible _____
10. awesome _____

C. Fill in the blank in each sentence below with the correct form of the word in parentheses.

1. John _____ (prefer) to eat meat for dinner.

2. We _____ (like) to go snowboarding in the winter.

3. Mr. and Mrs. Wilson _____ (want) to travel to America.

4. My sister _____ (enjoy) watching horror movies.

5. I _____ (hate) to kill spiders.

6. My neighbors _____ (prefer) to stay at home on Saturday nights.

7. Sam and Brian's favorite cartoon character _____ (be) Pokemon.

8. My favorite movies _____ (be) "Lion King" and "Gone with the Wind."

9. She _____ (like) bowling best.

10. My brother _____ (want) to be an exchange student in the U.S.

IV. Unit 4 Good Habits and Bad Habits

A. Ask your partner the following questions. Write down your partner's answers in full sentences.

1. Do you smoke? "_____"

2. Does your best friend smoke? "_____"

3. Do you get enough sleep? "_____"

4. How long did you sleep last night? "_____"

5. Does your mother get enough sleep? "_____"

6. Do you exercise? "_____"

7. Does your father exercise? "_____"

8. Do you eat a lot of fatty food? "_____"

9. Does your family eat a lot of fatty food? "_____"

10. Do you spend a lot of time outdoors? "_____"

B. Ask your partner these questions. Complete his/her answers on the lines. Use expressions like **"once a day,"** **"twice a week,"** **"every day,"** **"almost never,"** and **"sometimes"** in your answers. Then report each other's partner's answers to your group.

1. How often do you eat fast food? He/She _____

2. How often do you exercise? He/She _____

3. How often do you spend time outdoors? He/She _____

4. How often do you do sports? He/She _____

5. How often do you drink soda? He/She _____

C. Change partners in your group and ask your new partner these questions. Write his/her answers in full sentences. **Write out the numbers in words.**

1. What time is it now? _____
2. What time do your classes finish today? _____
3. What time do you go home today? _____
4. What time do you take the bus or train after school? _____
5. What time do you usually have dinner? _____
6. What time does your first lesson begin? _____
7. Do you have a part-time job? _____
8. (If yes to #7:) What time does your job start? _____
9. What time do you usually go to bed? _____
10. What time is it now? _____

Unit 5 Summer and Fun

I. Warm-Up:

A. Finish the short conversations below by matching the questions on the left with the answers on the right. Work with a partner.

_____ 1. Did you have a nice summer?   a. I came back last week.
_____ 2. What did you do?   b. I went with a friend.
_____ 3. Where did you go?   c. Yes, I did. I went to the beach every day.
_____ 4. When did you come back?   d. Yes, I did. New York was great.
_____ 5. How long were you there?   e. I was there for 10 days.
_____ 6. Who did you go with?   f. It was fun.
_____ 7. Did you have a summer job?   g. I enjoyed meeting my old high-school friends.
_____ 8. How was it?   h. I stayed in a hotel.
_____ 9. Did you enjoy your trip to America?   i. Yes, I worked in a restaurant.
_____ 10. Where did you stay?   j. I went to Disneyland.

B. Now practice the short conversations with your partner.

II. Vocabulary:

Look at the "Across" and "Down" crossword puzzle clues below. Fill in the blank in each clue with the past tense form of one of the verbs in this box. Write the words in the proper places in the puzzle. The first one has been done for you.

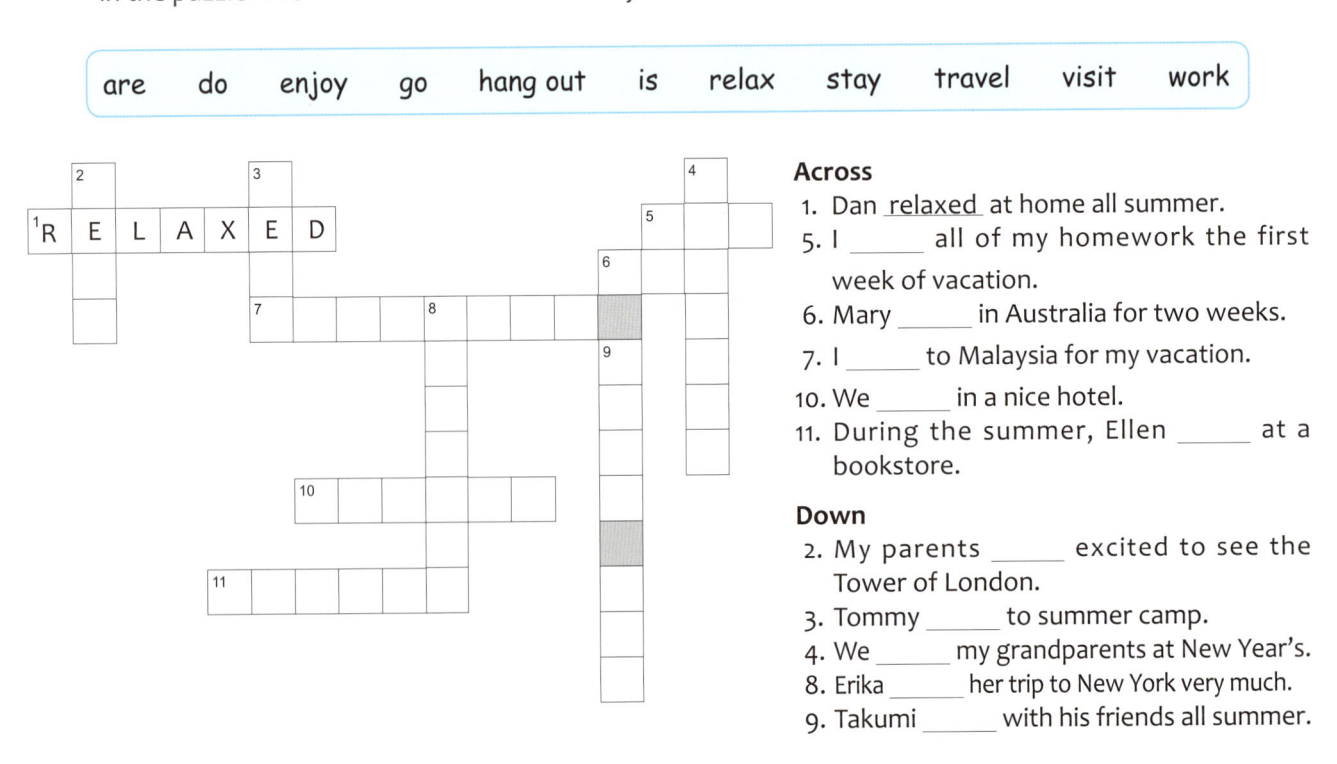

> are   do   enjoy   go   hang out   is   relax   stay   travel   visit   work

Across
1. Dan _relaxed_ at home all summer.
5. I _____ all of my homework the first week of vacation.
6. Mary _____ in Australia for two weeks.
7. I _____ to Malaysia for my vacation.
10. We _____ in a nice hotel.
11. During the summer, Ellen _____ at a bookstore.

Down
2. My parents _____ excited to see the Tower of London.
3. Tommy _____ to summer camp.
4. We _____ my grandparents at New Year's.
8. Erika _____ her trip to New York very much.
9. Takumi _____ with his friends all summer.

III. Dialogue:

A. Today is the first day back to school after the summer break. Mr. Wilson is asking the students about their summer vacations. Fill in the blanks as you listen to their discussion.

Mr. Wilson: Good morning, class. Welcome back to school. Did you have a nice summer (1) _____?

Students: Yes, we did.

Mr. Wilson: That's good to hear. My family and I went abroad. We (2) _____ to Finland for two weeks. It was beautiful. Did any of you take a (3) _____?

Takumi: I (4) _____ my relatives in the U.K. for 10 days. Then, after I got back, I (5) _____ at a summer camp for children with special needs.

Mr. Wilson: It sounds like you had a busy summer.

Erika: I went to the U.S. I (6) _____ in New York for a week. My friend Yurika and I went together. It was so much fun. When I (7) _____, I had a summer job at a restaurant.

Mr. Wilson: Did you (8) _____ a musical on Broadway?

Erika: Of course! It was wonderful!

Mr. Wilson: What about you, Yusuke?

Yusuke: I mostly (9) _____ at home, went to Disneyland a couple of times, and (10) _____ with some of my friends.

Mr. Wilson: So you enjoyed your vacation, too. Well everyone, back to work. Let's get started.

B. Make groups of four people. Practice the dialogue four times, changing roles each time.

Unit 5 Summer and Fun 51

IV. Check Your Understanding:

Work with a partner. Take turns asking and answering these questions about the dialogue. Write the answers on the lines in full sentences.

1. Where did Mr. Wilson and his wife go?

   _____

2. How long did they stay there?

   _____

3. What did Takumi do after his trip?

   _____

4. Did Erika travel to the U. S. by herself?

   _____

5. Who did Yusuke hang out with?

   _____

V. Conversation Check:

What did YOU do during the summer vacation? Work with a partner. Ask and answer the questions below. Write your partner's answers on the lines.

Student A: What did you do during summer vacation?

Student B: I _____

Student A: How long did you stay there?

Student B: I stayed there for _____

Student A: Who did you go with?

Student B: I went with _____

Student A: What did you see?

Student B: I saw _____

VI. Asking for More Information:

Ask five other classmates what they did during summer vacation. Write the information in the boxes.

Classmates' Names	Where?	Who?	How long?	What/see?
1.				
2.				
3.				
4.				
5.				

VII. Grammar Check:

Most verbs can be changed to past tense by simply adding "-ed" to the present tense form. But many verbs are "irregular," which means that to make the past tense, the spelling or maybe just the pronunciation changes.

A. Look at the verbs in this box. Then fill in the blank in each sentence below with the past tense form of the correct verb.

| buy | come | meet | think | eat | leave | hear | bring | listen | feel | walk | make |

1. Yusuke _____ carefully to the professor's lecture.
2. They _____ to the city library because they needed the exercise.
3. Erika _____ Yurika at the airport three hours before their flight.
4. Alice _____ her history book on the table.
5. Takumi _____ to class five minutes late.
6. My mother _____ me a cake for my birthday.
7. Yesterday, we _____ at that new Chinese restaurant.
8. I _____ that class was canceled this morning, but I was wrong.
9. Last week, Mr. Wilson _____ a new car.
10. The students quickly sat down when they _____ the teacher coming.
11. My friend Donna _____ her electronic dictionary to class.
12. Yusuke _____ sick when he woke up this morning.

B. Look at these examples of how the past tense of a verb is used in negative sentences and questions.

Past Tense Sentence	Negative	Question
He *went* to Paris.	He *didn't go* to Paris.	*Did* he *go* to Paris?
They *watched* TV.	They *didn't watch* TV.	*Did* they *watch* TV?
She *was* the fastest runner.	She *wasn't* the fastest runner.	*Was* she the fastest runner?
We *were* late for class.	We *weren't* late for class.	*Were* we late for class?

Now, fill in the blank in each sentence below to make a question or negative sentence.

1. We _____ (not) go anywhere yesterday.

2. _____ you finish your report?

3. They _____ (not) at the party last week.

4. _____ Takumi happy with his test score?

5. _____ you watch the drama on TV last night?

6. _____ we the first ones to finish our reports?

7. Erika _____ (not) want a present for her birthday.

8. I _____ (not) in class this morning because I missed the train.

9. _____ Yusuke meet his girlfriend last night?

10. We were so happy because the teacher _____ (not) give us any homework.

VIII. Look At This:

Look at this list of activities people often do during summer vacation. Can you think of any other activities? Write two more activities that you like to do.

> travel   relax at home   go abroad
> visit relatives   play (baseball)   go (swimming, hiking, etc.)
> watch fireworks   have a summer job   go to summer camp
> have a (picnic, barbecue party, etc.)   hang out with friends

1. _____

2. _____

IX. Conversation Practice:

Work with a partner. Use what you have learned in this unit to make a conversation about your summer vacation. Then practice the conversation with your partner, once as Student A and then again as Student B.

Student A: _____

Student B: _____

Student A: _____

Student B: _____

Student A: _____

Student B: _____

Student A: _____

Student B: _____

Student A: _____

Student B: _____

Student A: _____

Student B: _____

Unit 6   Here and There

I. Warm-up:

Fill in the blank in each sentence below with a word or phrase from this box.

> supermarket   bank   department stores   pharmacy   travel agency
> double-decker   convenience stores   post office   coffee shop   library

1. I need to go to the _____ to get some pounds (£).
2. You can buy tickets for the tour bus at the _____.
3. My mother buys all our food in the _____ on the corner.
4. I need some medicine for my cold. Where is the nearest _____?
5. I'm going to the _____. Do you have any books to take back?
6. In the UK, the _____ are not open 24 hours a day.
7. It's really cold. Let's go to a _____ and have a hot drink.
8. London is famous for its big, red, _____ buses.
9. Is there a _____ near here? I need to get some stamps for these postcards to Japan.
10. _____ sell everything from furniture to clothing.

II. Vocabulary:

All the words in the box above (in Section I) are hidden in the puzzle below. Find and circle each word. Work with a partner. The words can be vertical, horizontal, or diagonal. They may also be separated.

C	D	E	P	A	R	T	M	E	N	T	S
P	O	S	T	O	F	F	I	C	E	E	T
H	U	N	U	T	R	A	V	E	L	A	O
A	B	B	V	B	K	N	B	A	P	G	R
R	L	L	V	E	L	C	O	F	F	E	E
M	E	E	O	E	N	I	R	E	E	N	S
A	D	D	P	P	N	I	B	M	N	C	H
C	E	S	U	P	E	R	E	R	Y	Y	O
Y	C	M	A	R	K	E	T	N	A	O	P
A	K	K	K	F	I	C	E	N	C	R	K
G	E	E	B	A	N	K	M	R	C	E	Y
E	R	R	A	G	L	S	T	O	R	E	S

56

III. Dialogue:

A. During the summer vacation, Takumi stayed with his relatives in the U.K. This is a conversation Takumi had with his English grandmother. He calls her "Grandma." As you listen to their conversation, fill in the blanks.

Takumi: Grandma! I want to (1) _____ some Japanese yen (2) _____ pounds. Is there a bank near here?

Grandma: No. The nearest one is in the (3) _____ _____.

Takumi: How do I get there? Can I walk there?

Grandma: No, you can't. It's too far. You can (4) _____ the bus.

Takumi: Which bus do I take?

Grandma: The number 12. Go out of the house and turn (5) _____. Go to the bus stop (6) _____ _____ _____ near the gas station and wait for the number 12. It's a yellow (7) _____-_____ bus.

Takumi: Where do I (8) _____ _____?

Grandma: That's easy! It's the (9) _____ stop. The bus terminal is (10) _____ the town center.

B. Practice the dialogue twice with a partner, changing roles each time.

IV. Check Your Understanding:

Work with a partner. Take turns asking and answering these questions about the dialogue. Write your partner's answers on the lines in full sentences.

1. Why did Takumi want to go to the bank?
2. Where is the nearest bank?
3. How did Takumi get to the bank?
4. Where is the bus stop?
5. Where does he get off?

Unit 6 Here and There 57

V. Conversation Check:

A. Look at the tables below. Repeat the questions and answers after your teacher.

Questions:

Is there	a bank	near here?
	a coffee shop	around here?
Are there	any supermarkets	near your house?
	any restaurants	near the university?

Answers:

Yes, there is.	It's	next to the library.
No, there isn't.	It's	in the town center.
Yes, there are.	There's one	between the bank and the park.
No, there aren't.	There are some	in the next town.

B. Work with a partner to make up several short conversations of your own. Use these conversation patterns.

A: Is there a _____ around here?

B: Yes, there is. It's _____. (No, there isn't. There's one _____.)

A: Are there any _____ near your house?

B: Yes. There's one _____. (No, there aren't. There's one _____.)

VI. Asking for More Information:

A. There are many ways to ask for directions. In Parts I – V we learned to ask:

> **Is there a bank near here?**
>
> OR:
>
> **Is there a restaurant around here?**

To be more polite, you could also ask:

> **Excuse me, but where is the nearest station?**
>
> OR:
>
> **Could you tell me where the nearest station is, please?**

B. When we don't understand or cannot hear what the other person is saying, we can ask him or her to repeat it using any of the following:

> Pardon me?
> Pardon me, but could you say that again, please?
> I'm sorry, but could you speak more slowly, please?
> Excuse me, but could you repeat that, please?

Work with a partner. Practice this conversation several times, substituting words/phrases from the box above and the boxes below for the underlined parts.

Erika: Excuse me, but where is the nearest <u>post office</u>, please?
John: <u>Pardon me</u>?
Erika: Is there a <u>post office</u> near here?
John: Sure, there's one <u>across from</u> the <u>supermarket</u>.

> post office   gym   bookstore   Internet café   ATM
> travel agency   library   supermarket   restroom   pool

> near   next to   across from   on the right   behind
> in front of   on the left   between the _____ and the _____

VII. Grammar Check:

Fill in each blank with the correct form of the "be" verb.

1. Excuse me, but _____ there any good restaurants near here?
2. There _____ a library across from the station.
3. There _____ an Internet cafe next to the bookstore.
4. Let's go to a coffee shop. There _____ two good ones on the corner.
5. Where _____ the station?
6. _____ you in the bookstore? I can't find you.
7. I need to take out some money from an ATM. Where _____ the nearest bank?
8. The nearest travel agency _____ in the city center.
9. Pardon me, but _____ there a restroom near here?
10. _____ there any computer repair shops in this area?

Unit 6   Here and There   59

VIII. Look At This:

Look at the map below. Work with a partner, asking each other where certain places are located. Student A asks about the places in Box A. Student B asks about the places in Box B. Write the locations on the lines.

Example:

Student A: Where's the station?

Student B: It's across from the library.

Box A   (Student A)

post office	
gym	
bookstore	
internet cafe	
ATM	

Box B   (Student B)

travel agency	
library	
supermarket	
restroom	
pool	

60

IX. Conversation Practice:

Work with a partner. Use what you have learned in this unit and the map on page 60 to make a conversation. Take turns asking for and giving directions to the places on the map.

Student A: _____

Student B: _____

Student A: _____

Student B: _____

Student A: _____

Student B: _____

Student A: _____

Student B: _____

Student A: _____

Student B: _____

Student A: _____

Student B: _____

Unit 7   Giving and Receiving

I. Warm-up:

A. Finish the short conversations below by matching the questions/comments on the left with the responses on the right. Work with a partner.

1. I'm 19 today!
2. I'm getting married next year.
3. How much did your coat cost?
4. How many CDs did you buy?
5. What did you buy for your friend?
6. How much did you spend on your trip?
7. What did you give your mother for Mother's Day?
8. How much New Year's money did you get?
9. How many presents did you get for Christmas?
10. This shirt is too big.

a. I bought three. They were cheap.
b. I didn't spend much. It was inexpensive.
c. Congratulations! When?
d. Do you want a smaller one?
e. Happy Birthday!
f. I couldn't find anything suitable for her.
g. I got two big, expensive ones.
h. It was only 10,000 yen. It was reasonable.
i. I got 40,000 yen in one envelope.
j. I bought her some cups and saucers.

B. Now practice the short conversations with your partner.

II. Vocabulary:

Look at the clues for the crossword puzzle below. Each clue describes one of the words in this box. Write the words in the proper places in the puzzle. Work with a partner.

cheap   envelope   expensive   inexpensive   married
present   reasonable   saucers   spend   suitable

Across
1. I _____ most of my money on clothes.
2. cheap
4. small plates that go under cups
6. container for a letter
8. After I graduate, I plan to get _____ to my boyfriend.
9. Inexpensive

Down
1. Carnations are a _____ gift for a Mother's Day present.
3. A good price for a product
5. A high price
7. A gift

III. Dialogue:

A. Takumi and Erika meet at a department store. As you listen to their conversations, fill in the blanks.

Erika: Happy Birthday, Takumi! Here's a small (1) _____ for you.
Takumi: Thanks, Erika. You remembered my birthday! May I open it?
Erika: Sure. I hope you like it.
Takumi: Wow, a book on computer games. It's what I've always (2) _____!
Erika: I thought you'd like it.
Takumi: I really do. Thanks again.

* *

Takumi: Erika, my sister's getting (3) _____ next month …
Erika: (4) _____!
Takumi: Thanks. I'd like to buy her a wedding present. Could you help me?
Erika: Sure. How much do you want to (5) _____?
Takumi: About 10,000 yen.
Erika: How about some cups and saucers? There is a box of nice ones over there.
Takumi: How much do they cost?
Erika: 15,400 yen. They're a bit (6) _____.
Takumi: How many are in the box?
Erika: Five. Why don't you just buy three cups and saucers? You can get three for (7) _____ yen. That's (8) _____.
Takumi: You're right. Good idea!

* *

Erika: You're going to give her an (9) _____ of wedding money, too, aren't you?
Takumi: No, her husband-to-be is American, and they don't give money for wedding presents in America.
Erika: Really! What do they give? Just gifts?
Takumi: Yes, and do you know that American men give women chocolates on Valentine's Day? A big box of chocolates! A lot of chocolates!
Erika: Wow! I love chocolate. Will you buy ME some on Valentine's Day?
Takumi: Well, we're in Japan, so we can just give each other (10) _____ bars of chocolate.
Erika: If you say so. Now, let's go buy those cups and saucers.

B. Practice the dialogues twice with a partner, changing roles each time.

IV. Check Your Understanding:

Work with a partner. Take turns asking and answering these questions about the dialogues. Write the answers on the lines in full sentences.

1. What did Erika give Takumi for his birthday?

   _____

2. How much money does Takumi want to spend on his sister's wedding present?

   _____

3. How many cups are in the box?

   _____

4. How much do three cups and saucers cost?

   _____

5. Do people in America give money for wedding presents?

   _____

6. What will Takumi and Erika give each other for Valentine's Day?

   _____

V. Conversation Check:

Work with a partner. Fill in each blank below with a suitable noun. Then ask your partner the question. Write your partner's answers on the lines.

1. How many _____s do you have? (countable noun)

   _____

2. How much _____ do you have? (uncountable noun)

   _____

3. How much did your _____ cost?

   _____

4. How much did you spend on _____ this month?

   _____

VI. Asking for More Information:

Ask your partner these questions. Write his/her answers in full sentences.

1. How much New Year's money do you usually get?

2. How many CDs do you have?

3. What DVDs do you have?

4. How much did your shoes cost?

5. How many stuffed animals do you have at home?

6. How much do you pay for your cell phone per month?

7. How much did you spend on clothes this month?

8. Do you prefer fashionable shoes or comfortable shoes?

9. Did you buy anything this month?

10. What present would you give someone who is getting married?

VII. Grammar Check:

Fill in each blank below with **"a,"** **"some,"** **"any,"** **"much,"** **"many,"** or **"a lot of."** (It's OK to use a word or phrase more than once.)

1. I bought _____ bicycle last week.

2. We didn't get _____ presents for Christmas last year.

3. My girlfriend gave me _____ chocolate for Valentine's Day.

4. How _____ friends did you have when you were in high school?

5. Did you receive _____ letter from a friend?

6. You don't have _____ money to buy a present for your boyfriend, do you?

7. I don't know how _____ money he has in his wallet.

8. Did she get _____ chocolate at the store?

9. He doesn't have _____ computer of his own.

10. They didn't buy _____ ice cream at the convenience store today.

11. I'm so happy. I finally passed the test and got _____ driver's license!

12. He's excited because he got _____ good news from home.

13. How _____ information can you get on the Internet?

14. I have _____ friends at this school.

VIII. Look At This:

On this and the next page are the dates of some holidays in Japan, the US, and the UK. Write the names of the holidays in English next to the numbers. Work in a group.

	Japanese Holidays	American Holidays	British Holidays
January 1	1.	1.	1.
February 14	2.	2.	2.
March 3	3.	X	X
March 17	X	St. Patrick's Day	St. Patrick's Day
a Sunday in March or April	X	Easter	Easter
April 29	Showa Day	X	X
May 5	4.	X	X
1st Monday in May	X	X	Bank Holiday
2nd Sunday in May	5.	5.	X
a Sunday in March or April	X	X	Mothering Sunday
Last Monday in May	X	Memorial Day	Spring Bank Holiday
1st or 2nd Saturday in June	X	X	Queen's Official Birthday
3rd Sunday in June	6.	6.	X
July 4	X	Independence Day	X

Unit 7 Giving and Receiving

3rd Monday in July	Marine Day	X	X
Middle of August (July)	Obon/Return of the Souls Day	X	August Bank Holiday
1st Monday in September	X	Labor Day	X
3rd Monday in September	Respect for the Aged Day	X	X
Around September 23	7.	7.	7.
2nd Monday in October	8.	Columbus Day	X
October 31	(Halloween)	Halloween	X
November 3	Cultural Day	X	X
November 23	Labor Thanksgiving Day	X	X
4th Thursday in November	X	Thanksgiving Day	X
December 23	The Emperor's Birthday	X	X
December 25	9.	9.	9.
December 26	X	X	Boxing Day
December 31	10.	10.	10.

68

IX. Conversation Practice:

Work with a partner. You and your partner are shopping at a store. (It can be any kind of store.) Use what you have learned in this unit to write a short conversation. Decide what you are going to buy, how much the items cost, who they are for, and so on. Then practice the conversation twice, changing roles each time.

Student A: _____

Student B: _____

Student A: _____

Student B: _____

Student A: _____

Student B: _____

Student A: _____

Student B: _____

Student A: _____

Student B: _____

Student A: _____

Student B: _____

Unit 8 Parties and Fashion

I. Warm-Up:

A. Finish the short conversations below by matching the questions/comments on the left with the responses on the right. Work with a partner.

_____ 1. What are you going to wear to the party?
_____ 2. Are you going to take the bus?
_____ 3. What a beautiful dress!
_____ 4. Where are you going to go tomorrow?
_____ 5. What are you going to do this weekend?
_____ 6. Are you going to get contact lenses?
_____ 7. I'm going to have a party on Friday night.
_____ 8. What are you going to buy?
_____ 9. Are you going to take a gift for Erika?
_____ 10. When are you going to finish your report?

a. I'm going to see a new movie with my boyfriend on Saturday.
b. I'm going to buy a new skirt.
c. Yes, I am. I look better without glasses.
d. No, I'm going to drive my car.
e. Yes, I'm going to give her some flowers.
f. I'm going to wear jeans.
g. I'm going to finish it tonight.
h. I'm going to go shopping tomorrow.
i. Thank you. It's my favorite.
j. That sounds great! Can I come?

B. Now practice the short conversations with your partner.

II. Vocabulary:

Unscramble the letters beneath the pictures below to make the names of items of clothing and accessories.

1. knietce
2. lealtw
3. sreds
4. danssal
5. iust
6. snaslesugs
7. sjaen
8. hTrtsi-
9. essho
10. hsrsot
11. tha
12. itsrh
13. sokcs
14. voselg
15. tgtsih
16. resup

III. Dialogue:

A. Takumi and Yusuke are in a department store. Takumi is trying to find something new to wear to a party. As you listen to their conversation, fill in the blanks.

Takumi: Look at those neckties! I like the one with the pink and purple (1) _____. What do you think?

Yusuke: Um ... well, I think the stripes are a little (2) _____. I prefer this navy blue one with the white (3) _____ _____.

Takumi: I don't really need a necktie anyway. I'm going to go to Erika's party on Saturday, and she said to dress (4) _____.

Yusuke: Erika's party, huh? How about one of these (5) _____?

Takumi: This one's cool. It has a necktie printed on it. But it's too big. Oh, here is a smaller one. I wear a (6) _____.

Yusuke: How much is it?

Takumi: Three thousand yen! That's too (7) _____! Let's go to the arcade instead.

Yusuke: What are you going to (8) _____ to the party?

Takumi: I'm going to wear (9) _____ and my (10) _____ shirt. I hate shopping!

B. Practice the dialogue twice with a partner, changing roles each time.

Unit 8 Parties and Fashion   71

IV. Check Your Understanding:

Work with a partner. Take turns asking and asking these questions about the dialogue. Write the answers on the lines in full sentences.

1. What does Yusuke think of the necktie with the pink and purple stripes?

2. Where is Takumi going to go?

3. Should Takumi dress formally or casually for Erika's party?

4. Is Takumi going to buy the shirt? Why or why not?

5. What is Takumi going to wear to the party?

V. Conversation Check:

There are several ways to express the future tense. One way is like this:

"be" verb + going to + verb

Work with a partner. Look at the examples in the box. Make up four true sentences of your own, two affirmative and two negative. Dictate them to your partner. Write your partner's "dictation" to you on the lines below.

Affirmative	Negative
I'm going to drive to Ibaraki next weekend.	I'm not going to visit my grandmother tomorrow.
I'm going to write an e-mail to my sister tonight.	I'm not going to go to the party on Saturday.

1.
2.
3.
4.

VI. Asking for More Information:

Ask your partner the questions below. Add three more questions of your own. Write your partner's answers in full sentences.

1. What are you going to do tonight?

2. What time are you going to eat dinner?

3. Where are you going to spend spring vacation?

4. What are you going to do this weekend?

5. When are you going to graduate from this school?

6. _____?

7. _____?

8. _____?

VII. Grammar Check:

A. Countable/Uncountable nouns: Some items of clothing are countable and some are uncountable.
When using countable nouns, we use the article "a" when they are singular. When using uncountable nouns, sometimes we use "some," or nothing. Look at these example:

Countable nouns	Uncountable nouns
a shirt	(some) pants
a dress	(some) shorts
a skirt	(some) tights

This is how we talk about more than one item of clothing:

Plural countable nouns	Plural uncountable nouns
two shirts	three pairs of pants

Work with a partner. You are going to a hot spring spa this weekend. You are going to leave on Friday night and come back on Sunday night. Make a list of the clothing items and accessories that you are going to take. You need to take 10 different items.

Example: I'm going to take two shirts, a skirt, some pants, ...

B. Adjectives: Here are some common words used to describe clothing. Look up any words you don't understand in your dictionary.

big – small	expensive – inexpensive	fancy – casual
long – short	loud – muted	formal – informal
tight – loose	inappropriate – appropriate	

These words describe patterns:

solid   polka dot   striped   checked (plaid)

Unscramble the words below to make correct sentences. Write the sentences on the lines.

1. me / is / it / like / I / purse / but / this / for / expensive / too

2. too / is / this / short / skirt

3. you / pants / are / long / those / too / for

4. the / checked / I / blue / like / and / shirt / white

5. formal / is / this / very / dress

Unit 8 Parties and Fashion 75

VIII. Look At This:

We wear different clothes for different occasions or situations. For example, if we are going to meet a friend, we might wear some jeans and a shirt; if we are going for a job interview, we would wear more formal clothes like a suit. Look at the situations below and decide what clothes you would wear for each.

1. You are going to the movies with your boy/girlfriend.

   I would wear / I'm going to wear _____

   _____

   _____

2. You are going to a graduation party.

   _____

   _____

3. You are going shopping with a friend.

   _____

   _____

4. You are going to relax at home.

   _____

   _____

5. You are going to a formal event such as a wedding reception.

   _____

   _____

IX. Conversation Practice:

Work with a partner. Use the words and expressions you have learned in this unit to complete the conversations below. Then practice the conversations with your partner, once as Student A, and then as Student B.

Student A: Hi. What are you going to do this weekend?

Student B: I'm going to _____

Student A: Really? That sounds _____.

(Who ~? What time ~? How long ~?)

_____?

Student B: _____

Student A: What are you going to wear?

Student B: I'm going to _____

Student A: Well, have a _____ time.

See you _____

Student B: _____

Review   Units 5 – 8

I.   Unit 5:   Summer and Fun

A. Use the hints below and the past tense to write complete questions. Work with a partner.

1. ... have a nice summer?

2. What ... do?

3. Where ... go?

4. How long ...?

5. Where ... stay?

6. ... visit ... family?

7. ... summer camp?

8. ... summer job?

B. Ask your partner the questions on page 78 and write his/her answers on the lines.

1. _____
2. _____
3. _____
4. _____
5. _____
6. _____
7. _____
8. _____

C. Fill in the blank in each sentence below with the correct past tense form of one of these verbs.

| feel | come | meet | think | bring | buy |

1. Mr. Wilson _____ to the lesson ten minutes late yesterday.
2. I was late because I _____ the class started at 9:30.
3. I _____ my father a new CD for Father's Day.
4. I _____ nervous when I started my new school.
5. Erika _____ her dictionary to class but she forgot her textbook.
6. Takumi _____ Erika at the bus stop.

II. Unit 6: Here and There

A. Look at the map in Unit 6 on page 60. With a partner, take turns asking and answering these questions.

1. Excuse me. Is there an Internet café near here?
   _____

2. Could you tell me where the nearest pharmacy is, please?
   _____

3. Is there a parking lot near the supermarket?
   _____

4. Are there any bookstores near here?
   _____

5. I want to buy a soda and a sandwich. Is there a shop near here?
   _____

B. Work with a partner. Look at the map again and write a sentence that contains each of these words or phrases. Imagine you are standing in front of the station.

1. next to _____

2. between _____

3. across from _____

4. near _____

5. on the right _____

6. on the left _____

7. in front of _____

8. behind _____

C. Fill in the blanks in these sentences with words/phrases from Unit 6.

1. The banks are closed now. You can get some money at the _____.

2. I want to send a letter to America. Is there a _____ near here?

3. You can buy pasta and tomato sauce at the _____ on the corner.

4. In Japan, the _____ are open 24 hours a day.

5. I need to go to the _____ to get some U.S. dollars.

6. Is the _____ still open? I want to borrow some more books.

7. I'm tired. Let's go to a _____ and have a cup of coffee.

8. Is there a _____ near the station? I need some cold medicine.

III. Unit 7: Giving and Receiving

A. Match the questions on the left with the answers on the right.

_____ 1. How much is that box of chocolates?   a. No, I didn't.

_____ 2. When is Valentine's Day?   b. I have about 30.

_____ 3. Did you get any presents for your birthday?   c. Two kilograms.

_____ 4. What did you give Erika for Valentine's Day?   d. It cost about ¥80,000.

_____ 5. How much rice did you buy?   e. Yes, he did.

_____ 6. How much did your computer cost?   f. Yes, I do. A lot!

_____ 7. How many CDs do you have?   g. It's on February 14th.

_____ 8. Did Takumi get a book on computer games?   h. It's ¥2,000.

_____ 9. How many pets do you have?   i. I gave her six roses.

_____ 10. Do you have a lot of clothes?   j. I have two cats.

B. Fill in the blank in each sentence below with "**a**," "**some**," or "**any**."

1. I didn't get _____ presents for my birthday.

2. I want _____ more sugar in my coffee.

3. Do you have _____ money in your pocket?

4. I bought _____ new computer last week.

5. Please go to the shop and buy _____ rice.

C. Fill in the blank in each sentence below with **"much," "many,"** or **"a lot of."**

1. There aren't _____ students in our class.

2. He doesn't have _____ money.

3. There is _____ rice in the bag.

4. There's too _____ salt in this soup.

5. We didn't get _____ presents for Christmas last year.

6. Don't eat too _____ snacks at the party!

7. I have _____ friends who live in Tokyo.

D. Ask your partner these questions. Write your his/her answers in full sentences.

1. How much did your shirt cost?

   _____

2. How many CDs do you have?

   _____

3. What did you get your mother for her birthday?

   _____

4. How much money did you spend this week?

   _____

5. How much does it cost you to get to school?

   _____

Review   Units 5-8

IV. Unit 8: Parties and Fashion

A. Work with a partner. Make short conversations by matching the questions/comments on the left with the responses on the right.

_____ 1. Are you going to take the train?
_____ 2. What color is Erika's new dress?
_____ 3. What are you going to do this Sunday?
_____ 4. I'm going to go to a karaoke party tonight.
_____ 5. Are you going to give Mr. Wilson a gift for his birthday?
_____ 6. What a beautiful suit!
_____ 7. When are you going to finish your report?
_____ 8. What are you going to wear to the party?

a. Yes. I'm going to bake him a cake.
b. Thank you. It's my favorite.
c. That sound's great! Can I come?
d. No, I'm going to take the bus.
e. I'm going to go shopping with my sister.
f. I'm going to finish it tonight.
g. It's blue with white polka dots.
h. I'm going to wear my new jeans.

B. Change these affirmative sentences into negative sentences, as in the example.

Example: I'm going to drive to Bay Town next weekend.
I'm not going to drive to Bay Town next weekend.

1. I'm going to eat dinner at about 7 o'clock tonight.

   _____

2. I'm going to take my driving test in the spring break.

   _____

3. I'm going to wear my jeans and a red checked shirt.

   _____

C. Ask your partner the questions below. Add two more questions of your own about future plans. Write your partner's answers in full sentences.

1. What are you going to wear to school tomorrow?

2. What are you going to have for dinner tonight?

3. _____?

4. _____?

Unit 9 Physical Education and Health

I. Warm-up:

A. Work with a partner. Decide which word, "**do**," "**go**," or "**play**," goes with the following sports. Write the correct word on each line. (We often substitute "**practice**" for "**do**.")

1. _____ sports
2. _____ baseball
3. _____ swimming
4. _____ track and field
5. _____ fishing
6. _____ tennis
7. _____ hiking
8. _____ judo
9. _____ dancing
10. _____ darts
11. _____ jogging
12. _____ gymnastics
13. _____ basketball
14. _____ karate
15. _____ soccer
16. _____ volleyball
17. _____ martial arts
18. _____ yoga

B. Now ask your partner about the sports he/she did in P.E. or in clubs in junior and senior high school. Use the example as a model for your questions. Write your partner's sports on the lines below.

Example:

A: What sports did you do or play in junior high school?
B: I played baseball, went swimming, ... in junior high school.
A: What sports did you do or play in high school?
B: I did judo, ... in high school.

You: (Junior high) _____

(High school) _____

Your Partner: (Junior high) _____

(High school) _____

II. Vocabulary:

Fill in the blank in each sentence below with the correct form of a word or phrase from this box. Work with a partner.

> break up   hip-hop   head start   two left feet   license
> P.E. (Physical Education)   female   compulsory   What's up   martial arts

1. I loved _____ classes in the gym when I was in high school.

2. In the summer, Ted's going to driving school to get his driver's _____.

3. If I read my new textbooks before the classes start, I'll get a good _____.

4. My boyfriend and I _____ because he moved far away and never wrote to me.

5. English is a _____ subject in junior and senior high schools in Japan.

6. My brother joined a _____ club, where he practiced kendo, judo and karate.

7. When Sally met her friend, she asked her, "_____?"

8. I have _____ when I try to dance.

9. In junior high school P.E. class, we learned to dance _____.

10. In elementary school, I had more _____ teachers than male teachers.

III. Dialogue:

A. Yusuke and Erika are talking on Friday after class. As you listen to their conversation, fill in the blanks.

Yusuke: Hi, Erika. (1) _____ _____?

Erika: Nothing much. I have a lot of homework this weekend, so I'm trying to get a (2) _____ _____ on it.

Yusuke: Oh, really? I was wondering if you'd like to go with me to watch a (3) _____ _____ tournament at the Budokan tomorrow.

Erika: Really?! What kind of tournament?

Yusuke: There are a few different martial arts. They'll do karate, judo, and kendo.

Erika: But what would your girlfriend think?

Yusuke: Well, we (4) _____ _____ last month.

Erika: Oh, I'm so sorry to hear that.

Yusuke: It's OK. We're just interested in different things.

Erika: What are you interested in?

Yusuke: Well, sports, of course. I like to go fishing, play baseball, and do judo.

Erika: I didn't know you were interested in judo.

Yusuke: Well, to get a teacher's (5) _____, we have to learn it in college. So I just started to practice it. And do you know, modern dance is also (6) _____ now for junior high gym classes?

Erika: Both male and (7) _____ teachers have to teach dance classes? What if you have (8) _____ _____ _____?

Yusuke: It could be folk dance, but most schools are choosing (9) _____-_____.

Erika: Well, I loved (10) _____ in school, so I'd love to go with you.

Yusuke: Terrific! How about we meet at Kudanshita Station at noon?

Erika: Sounds great! I'll have to do my homework on Sunday, I guess.

B. Practice the dialogue twice with a partner, changing roles each time.

IV. Check Your Understanding:

Work with a partner. Take turns asking and answering these questions about the dialogue. Write the answers on the lines in full sentences.

1. Why does Erika want to do her homework this weekend?

   _____

2. Where does Yusuke invite her to go?

   _____

3. What kind of martial arts will be performed at the Budokan?

   _____

4. What happened to Yusuke and his girlfriend?

   _____

5. What sports does Yusuke like to do?

   _____

6. What two things are compulsory now for junior high P.E. classes?

   _____

V. Conversation Check:

With a partner, complete the conversation below. Practice it a few times, changing roles until you can do it without reading it.

Student A: Hi _____. What's up?
Student B: Nothing much. _____
Student A: I was wondering if you'd like to _____
             _____
Student B: What about _____?
Student A: _____
Student B: What are you interested in?
Student A: _____
             How about you?
Student B: _____
Student A: How about we meet at _____?
Student B: _____

Unit 9   Physical Education and Health   89

VI. Asking for More Information:

What did you do in junior high and high school gym classes and clubs? Write your answers in the spaces for "you." Then talk to four classmates to find out what sports they did and what clubs they were in. Write their answers in the appropriate spaces. Use this example as a model.

Ask: "What did you do in junior high gym classes?" "What club were you in?"

Answer: "I played tennis, went swimming, ..." "I was in the volleyball club."

Names ↓	Junior High Gym?	Junior High Club?	High School Gym?	High School Club?
1. You				
2.				
3.				
4.				
5.				

VII. Grammar Check:

As we learned above, there are three basic verbs that are used to talk about sports; "**go**," "**play**," and "**do**." We use "go" with sports or activities that we go out to do: "go fishing," "go dancing," etc. We use "play" with sports/games that use a ball or other item (puck, shuttlecock, darts). We use "do" generally with the word "sports," as in: "What sport did you do in college?" (Here, we can also say "What sports did you play in college?) We also use "do" for martial arts: "do judo," "do karate." (We can also say "practice judo" or "practice karate.")

Work with a partner. Fill in the blank in each sentence below. Then read the sentences to each other.

1. My brother _____ American football in a college club.

2. We _____ folk dancing in our high school P.E. classes.

3. Do you like to _____ swimming in an indoor pool?

4. When I was little I _____ biking with my family.

5. My sister _____ aikido at a community center.

6. She _____ field hockey as an after-school activity when she was in junior high school.

7. In the summers, we often _____ tennis with our friends.

8. I _____ swimming every week when I was in elementary school.

9. Mariko doesn't like _____ hiking up mountains.

10. Jun _____ gymnastics in a school club.

VIII. Look At This:

Look at the list of things you may have learned about in health classes in junior high and high school. Look up those you don't understand in your dictionary. Ask your partner what he/she learned in school. Make a check mark [✓] next to each topic your partner or you learned about. Use this pattern:

Ask: "Did you learn about …?"

_____ nutrition	_____ diseases	_____ mental health
_____ calorie counting	_____ cholesterol	_____ sex education
_____ cancer	_____ heart disease	_____ stress management
_____ obesity	_____ addiction; smoking	_____ a healthy lifestyle

Ask your partner this question. Write his/her answers on the lines.

What other things did you learn in health classes?

_____

_____

_____

Unit 9 Physical Education and Health

IX. Conversation Practice:

Work with a partner. Use what you have learned in this unit to make a conversation about sports. Then practice with your partner, once as Student A and then again as Student B.

Student A: _____

Student B: _____

Student A: _____

Student B: _____

Student A: _____

Student B: _____

Student A: _____

Student B: _____

Student A: _____

Student B: _____

Student A: _____

Student B: _____

Student A: _____

Student B: _____

Student A: _____

Student B: _____

Unit 10 Nursery School and Day Care

I. Warm-up:

A. Finish the short conversations below by matching the questions on the left with the responses on the right. Work with a partner.

_____ 1. How old are the children in this class?
_____ 2. Did you go to nursery school?
_____ 3. How do the children come to school?
_____ 4. Do the children bring a packed lunch every day?
_____ 5. What are the hours at this day-care center?
_____ 6. Do you have to teach the children to read and write?
_____ 7. Do the children like the nursery school?
_____ 8. How many children are there in one class?
_____ 9. How do you like helping out at the kindergarten?
_____ 10. Do you do any volunteer work?

a. The hours are from 8:00 a.m. to 6:00 p.m.
b. Yes, I volunteer at a kindergarten.
c. No, I don't. They don't study subjects like that.
d. Yes, they do. Their favorite activity there is singing songs.
e. That depends on their ages. The younger ones have smaller classes.
f. They're all three years old.
g. They either walk or come on the school bus.
h. It's great. I really enjoy going there every day.
i. No, I didn't. I went to day care.
j. No, this nursery school serves lunch.

B. Now practice the short conversations with your partner.

II. Vocabulary:

Look up the words and phrases below in your English-Japanese dictionary. Write the Japanese meanings on the lines.

1. experience _____
2. to look forward to _____
3. guidelines _____
4. to discipline _____
5. manners _____
6. proper _____
7. behavior _____
8. to treat _____
9. to have favorites _____
10. to be fair _____
11. activity _____
12. to encourage _____
13. variety _____
14. to contribute _____
15. opportunity _____
16. to scold _____

III. Dialogue:

A. Erika just arrived at an international nursery school near her university. She will start volunteering here next week. Today, she is having a meeting with the principal of the school, Mrs. Stewart, to discuss her duties. As you listen to their conversation, fill in the blanks.

Mrs. Stewart: Please come in, Ms. Kaneko. I'm glad to meet you.

Erika: Thank you. Please call me Erika. I'm very excited to be here.

Mrs. Stewart: Is this your first (1) _____ volunteering at a nursery school?

Erika: Yes, it is. It has always been my dream to work with children, so I'm really (2) _____ _____ _____ this chance.

Mrs. Stewart: I see. Well, today I would like to give you a few (3) _____ to follow.

Erika: Is it all right if I take notes?

Mrs. Stewart: Of course. First of all, you don't have to (4) _____ the children. The teacher will teach the children manners and proper (5) _____.

Erika: I understand.

Mrs. Stewart: Next, please remember that you have to (6) _____ all the children equally. It's easy to have favorites, but we want all of the teachers to be fair.

Erika: Yes, of course.

Mrs. Stewart: Finally, you will have to help the teacher with the games and (7) _____. Please remember that we prefer to use the Montessori method here.

Erika: Excuse me, what does that mean?

Mrs. Stewart: It means that we like to (8) _____ independence and freedom. We want the children to enjoy a variety of activities that include singing, dancing, and outdoor activities. Please (9) _____ any ideas you have to the teacher. Do you have any questions?

Erika: No, I don't think so. This is going to be a fantastic learning (10) _____ for me.

Mrs. Stewart: I'm sure it will be. See you next Monday.

Erika: Thank you. See you then.

B. Practice the dialogue twice with a partner, changing roles each time.

IV. Check Your Understanding:

Work with a partner. Take turns asking and answering these questions about the dialogue. Write the answers on the lines in full sentences.

1. Where is Erika going to volunteer?
   _____

2. Is it all right if Erika scolds the children?
   _____

3. Why does Mrs. Stewart want Erika to treat all the children equally?
   _____

4. What kinds of activities do the children do?
   _____

5. When will Erika start volunteering at the nursery school?
   _____

V. Conversation Check:

Complete the conversation below with a partner. Practice it a few times, changing roles until you can do it without reading it.

Student A: May I ask you some questions?
Student B: Sure.
Student A: Did you go to nursery school or day care when you were a child?
Student B: _____
Student A: What kind of activities did you do?
Student B: _____
Student A: What was your favorite activity?
Student B: _____
Student A: Do you still have any friends from then?
Student B: _____
Student A: OK. Thank you.
Student B: _____

VI. Asking for More Information:

First, write your own answers to the five questions below. Then take turns asking and answering the questions with a new partner. Write your partner's answers in the boxes.

	Questions	Your Answers	Your Partner's Answers
1.	Have you ever done any volunteer work?		
2.	What kind of volunteer work would you like to do?		
3.	How old were you when you started going to some kind of school or day care?		
4.	Who was your favorite teacher?		
5.	Do you have any experience working with children?		

VII. Grammar Check:

When talking about something we must do, we often say "**have to.**" Look at the table below and then fill in the blanks in the sentences that follow with the correct answers, as in the example. Make sure you use "have to."

Affirmative (yes)			Negative (no)		
I You We They It	have to	wake up early tomorrow.	I You We They It	don't have to	wake up early tomorrow.

A. Example: (He / go to school / tomorrow — No) He doesn't have to go to school tomorrow.

1. (I / do my homework / tonight — Yes)

2. (He / call his mother / this week — No)

3. (They / go shopping / today — No)

4. (We / clean our room / this weekend — Yes)

5. (Erika / scold the children / at the nursery school — No)

B. Now write two sentences, one affirmative and one negative about what you have to/don't have to do this weekend. Use "have to."

1.

2.

Unit 10   Nursery School and Day Care   97

VIII. Look At This:

Erika really enjoyed the time she spent volunteering at the nursery school. Here is a timetable of the activities she helped with. Read the timetable and use your dictionary to look up the meanings of the words you don't understand. Work with your partner to think of some activities to fill in the last five boxes.

Time	Activity	Erika had to
8:45 a.m. — 9:00 a.m.	Arrival time	help the children take off their coats and shoes and say goodbye to Mommy and Daddy
9:00 a.m. — 9:30 a.m.	Circle Time	sing songs / read stories / play the piano
9:30 a.m. — 10:30 a.m.	Outdoor free play	help the children climb on the jungle gym / play in the sand box / go on the slide / play on the swings
10:30 a.m. — 11:30 a.m.	Table-top activities	give out paper and paints / crayons / help the children use scissors / fold origami
11:30 a.m. — 12:00 p.m.	Tidy up time, toilet and diaper time, and washing hands to get ready for lunch time	show the children how to tidy up / wipe the tables / put the toys away / help the children use the toilet / wash their hands / change the younger children's diapers
12:30 a.m. — 12:45 p.m.	Lunchtime	help the children eat their lunch using spoons and forks or chopsticks / supervise tidying up after lunch
12:45 p.m. — 1:00 p.m.	Quiet time	read stories to older children / supervise nap-time for the younger children
1:00 p.m. — 2:00 p.m.	Outdoor free play	
2:00 p.m. — 2:50 p.m.	Table-top activities	
2:50 p.m. — 3:30 p.m.	TV time/singing/dancing	
3:30 p.m. — 4:00 p.m.	Getting ready to go home	
4:00 p.m. — 4:15 p.m.	Home time	

IX. Conversation Practice:

Continue to work with a partner. Use what you have learned in this unit and the timetable on the previous page to make a conversation. Erika (A) is talking to her classmate (B) about her volunteer work at the nursery school. Erika's friend is asking about what activities Erika had to do and at what time they started and ended. When you finish, practice twice with your partner, changing roles each time.

Student A: _____

Student B: _____

Student A: _____

Student B: _____

Student A: _____

Student B: _____

Student A: _____

Student B: _____

Student A: _____

Student B: _____

Student A: _____

Student B: _____

Student A: _____

Student B: _____

Student A: _____

Student B: _____

Unit 11   Educating and Caring

I.   Warm-up:

A.   Finish the short conversations below by matching the questions on the left with the responses on the right. Work with a partner.

_____   1. Hello. What can I do for you?   a. We have to leave at 7 a.m.

_____   2. What do we need to bring to class?   b. Yes, I learned to sign at school.

_____   3. Can you eat with a knife and fork?   c. Yes, she does.

_____   4. When do we have to leave?   d. Yes, I can, but not very well.

_____   5. What should I do with my medicine?   e. Yes, I do.

_____   6. Does Anna need a hearing aid?   f. Can you help me read this letter, please?

_____   7. Do you go to a special-education school?   g. You need everything on this list.

_____   8. How much money should I bring?   h. No, I'm sorry you can't. Let's wait for
_____   9. Can you use sign language?   the next one.

_____   10. Can I get on this bus with my   i. You should give it to the teacher to keep.
            wheelchair?   j. About 3,000 yen.

B.   Now practice the short conversations with your partner.

II. Vocabulary:

Fill in the blank in each sentence below with the correct form of a word or phrase from this box. Work with a partner.

> eating utensil   wheelchair   medication   diaper   lunch bag
> backpack   change of clothes   sign language   Braille   toiletry kit

1. We are going to stay overnight, so we need two _____.

2. Put this ice-pack in your _____. It'll keep the food fresh.

3. A lot of the children in this class need special cups and _____.

4. Don't forget to give Mark's _____ to his teacher. She will keep it for him.

5. My new friend at university is deaf, so I decided to learn _____.

6. You have to bring a _____ with soap, toothpaste, a toothbrush, a face towel, and a hair brush.

7. The school usually has plenty of _____, but you should bring your own if you can.

8. I think you're going to need a bigger _____. You have too many things to fit into that small one.

9. Excuse me. Is there a _____ information sign at this station?

10. We'll need two assistants tomorrow. Akira's _____ is too heavy for one person to manage.

III. Dialogue:

A. Mr. Endo, the English teacher at Akebono Special Education School, has an appointment with Mrs. Dean, the mother of one of his students, Mark. Mrs. Dean comes from Canada, and she doesn't speak or read Japanese very well yet. As you listen to their conversation, fill in the blanks.

Mr. Endo: Hello, Mrs. Dean. Please come in and sit down. What (1) _____ _____ _____ for you?

Mrs. Dean: Good afternoon. Thank you for seeing me. It's this letter about the (2) _____ _____ to Tokyo. Can you help me read it?

Mr. Endo: Of course. Which part can't you read?

Mrs. Dean: It's this part here. It's the list of things we need to put in his bag, I think.

Mr. Endo: I see. Well, he has to bring a (3) _____ _____ _____ and a raincoat. It also says he needs to bring diapers and any special (4) _____ equipment he needs.

Mrs. Dean: He can use the toilet by himself now, so he doesn't need (5) _____. What about his medicine?

Mr. Endo: It says here that students have to bring their (6) _____ and give them to the teacher. He also has to bring a (7) _____ _____ with something to drink and some snacks. Mark can eat regular food, can't he?

Mrs. Dean: Yes, he's fine, but he needs his special (8) _____ _____. It's difficult for him to use ordinary ones. What does this say here?

Mr. Endo: It says he should bring a (9) _____ _____ so he can wash his hands and face. Don't forget the last thing!

Mrs. Dean: What's that?

Mr. Endo: Pocket money. Everybody is allowed to bring ¥2,000 to spend. We like them to practice buying things in a shop. It helps them to be more (10) _____.

Mrs. Dean: Oh, I see! Well, I think that's all. Thank you so much for helping me.

Mr. Endo: Don't mention it. Just call the office if you need anything. We'll see you on Wednesday.

Mrs. Dean: Yes. Mark's really looking forward to it.

B. Practice the dialogue twice with a partner, changing roles each time.

IV. Check Your Understanding:

Work with a partner. Take turns asking and answering these questions about the dialogue. Write the answers on the lines in full sentences.

1. How did Mr. Endo help Mark's mother?

   _____

2. Does Mark need to bring any diapers?

   _____

3. What do the students have to do with their medications?

   _____

4. Can Mark eat regular food?

   _____

5. Why does Mark need special eating utensils?

   _____

6. How much pocket money can everybody bring?

   _____

V. Conversation Check:

What do you need to take with you when you are going on a trip? Work with your partner. Look at the different "trips" below and make lists of the things you would need to bring for each. Write at least three things.

What would you need to bring if you were going on …

1. … a picnic?

   "You need to bring _____."

2. … a one-day school trip?

   _____

3. … an overnight school trip?

   _____

4. … a trip with a disabled person?

   _____

Unit 11 Educating and Caring 103

VI. Asking For More Information:

Work with a group of four or five people. Ask the other students these questions. Write their answers on the lines.

- Was there a special-education classroom at your elementary school or junior high school? What was it called?

- What special education schools are there in your town?

Student 1:

_____

_____

Student 2:

_____

_____

Student 3:

_____

_____

Student 4:

_____

_____

VII. Grammar Check:

Ask your partner about what is **easy (for him/her) to do** and what is **difficult (for him/her) to do**. Look at the following examples.

Mark's teacher:	Mrs. Dean, is it difficult for Mark go to the restroom by himself?
Mark's mother:	Yes, it is. It's difficult for him to go alone. He needs a little help.
Erika:	Is it easy for you to get to school so early?
Takumi:	Yes, it is. It's easy for me because I always get up early anyway.

Use the patterns above to ask your partner questions with **easy (for you) to ...** and **hard (for you) to ...**
Use the boxes below to write his/her answers. Use your own ideas for the last four examples.

	Easy	Difficult	Reason
Drive a car			
Cook dinner			
Sing karaoke			
Use a wheel chair			

Your ideas:	Easy	Difficult	Reason
1.			
2.			
3.			
4.			

Unit 11 Educating and Caring

VIII. Look At This:

There are several different types of schools for children with special educational needs. Here is a list of some of the most common. Often two or more types of schools are combined into one facility.

A child may go to a school for the deaf.

a school for the blind

a school for the mentally disabled

a school for the physically disabled

a hospital school for very sick children

a school for children with emotional or psychological problems

a special education classroom at a regular school

Look at the disabilities listed below. Work with your partner to look up the meanings in a dictionary and then write them in Japanese. Then use the list above to write the type of school or schools these children might attend. If you don't know the answers, find out for homework.

Disability	Japanese	Type of School
Down's Syndrome		
Muscular Dystrophy		
Developmental Problems		
Spina Bifida		
Autism		
Visual Impairment (Blind)		
Hearing Impairment (Deaf)		
ADHD*		
Dyslexia and other LDs**		
Cerebral Palsy (CP)		

*ADHD (attention deficit hyperactivity disorder)
**LD (learning disability)

IX. Conversation Practice:

You and your partner are planning a summer camp for your English Conversation Club. One of the members is disabled and uses a wheelchair. Write a short conversation using what you have learned in this unit. First, decide what is difficult for your disabled friend to do and what special needs he/she has. Then practice the conversation twice, once as Student A and then as Student B.

Student A: Let's decide where to go for our summer camp.

Student B: Yes. Let's _____

Student A: _____

Student B: _____

Student A: _____

Student B: _____

Student A: _____

Student B: _____

Student A: _____

Student B: _____

Student A: _____

Student B: _____

Student A: _____

Student B: _____

Unit 12   Bullying and Other Problems

I. Warm-up:

A. Finish the short conversations below by matching the questions/comments on the left with the responses on the right. Work with a partner.

_____ 1. Good afternoon. Thank you for coming.
_____ 2. What's the problem?
_____ 3. I have a slight fever and my head hurts.
_____ 4. Has anything happened at school?
_____ 5. Is John being bullied?
_____ 6. Can you talk to the students about it?
_____ 7. Were you successful?
_____ 8. Did you let him stay home?
_____ 9. Were you absent last week?
_____ 10. Thank you for handling this. I feel much better now.

a. Yes, I'm afraid so. Some students are making fun of your son.
b. I'm sorry to hear that.
c. Yes, I will call a meeting tomorrow.
d. No, I attended class.
e. No, I made my son go to school.
f. Thank you for seeing me.
g. I'm glad I could help you. If you have any further problems, please come back.
h. Yes, we put an end to the bullying.
i. My son doesn't want to go to school. He's quite unhappy.
j. I think he is.

B. Now practice the short conversations with your partner.

II. Vocabulary:

Fill in the blank in each crossword puzzle clue below. Write the words in the proper places in the puzzle. Work with a partner.

Across
2. There was an incident of _____ at the school.
4. I wasn't _____ one time this year. I had perfect attendance.
5. He's not physically harmed, but he's sad, so his feelings are _____.
6. We have to _____ their fighting.
7. It's hard to _____ violent students.
8. If you have any _____ questions, ask me anytime.
9. She became rich and _____ in her business.

Down
1. He is _____ tired after the long trip.
3. I have a _____ headache, but it's not too bad.
4. Did you _____ the meeting this morning?
8. I had a _____ last night, but now my temperature is normal.

108

III. Dialogue:

A. Mrs. Wilson, Mr. Wilson's wife, visits Mr. Suzuki, their son's first grade teacher, to talk about their son. As you listen to their conversation, fill in the blanks.

Mr. Suzuki: Good afternoon, Mrs. Wilson. Thank you for coming.

Mrs. Wilson: Thank you for (1) _____ me, Mr. Suzuki.

Mr. Suzuki: I heard that you wanted to see me about a problem with your son.

Mrs. Wilson: Yes, that's right. John doesn't want to go to school these days. He often has a (2) _____ fever in the morning.

Mr. Suzuki: I'm sorry to (3) _____ that.

Mrs. Wilson: Sometimes I make him go to school, and other times I (4) _____ him stay home.

Mr. Suzuki: Yes. I see he's been (5) _____ quite a lot recently.

Mrs. Wilson: Has anything been happening at school?

Mr. Suzuki: I think some students have been (6) _____ him names since he started wearing glasses.

Mrs. Wilson: So, he's being (7) _____?

Mr. Suzuki: I don't know if I'd call it bullying. They are making fun of him, though.

Mrs. Wilson: But that is bullying! We have to put an end to this right away! Can you talk to your students about it?

Mr. Suzuki: Of course. I will call a meeting tomorrow and talk to all of the first graders.

Mrs. Wilson: Thank you very much. If it goes any (8) _____, someone could get hurt.

Mr. Suzuki: Yes, we've had to handle this (9) _____ _____ thing before.

Mrs. Wilson: Were you successful?

Mr. Suzuki: Yes, we were able to put an end to it, because we (10) _____ it early.

Mrs. Wilson: Thank you for your time, Mr. Suzuki.

Mr. Suzuki: I'm glad I could help. Thank you for coming. And if you ever have any other problems, please call me again. Goodbye.

B. Practice the dialogue twice with a partner, changing roles each time.

IV. Check Your Understanding:

Work with a partner. Take turns asking and answering these questions about the dialogue. Write the answers on the lines in full sentences.

1. Why did Mrs. Wilson meet Mr. Suzuki?

   _____

2. What often happens to John in the mornings?

   _____

3. What does Mrs. Wilson do when this happens?

   _____

4. How is John being bullied?

   _____

5. What is Mr. Suzuki going to do about the problem?

   _____

V. Conversation Check:

Imagine you are a parent talking with an elementary school teacher about your son's or daughter's problem. Complete the conversation below with a partner. Practice the conversation a few times, changing roles.

Teacher:	Good afternoon, Mrs./Mr./Ms. _____. Thank you for coming.
Parent:	Thank you for seeing me, Mr./Mrs./Ms. _____.
Teacher:	I heard that you wanted to see me about a problem with your _____.
Parent:	Yes, (problem) _____.
Teacher:	I'm sorry to hear that.
Parent:	(more about the problem) _____.
Teacher:	(teacher's idea about what the problem is) _____.
Parent:	(parent's question) _____.
Teacher:	(teacher's suggestion) _____.
Parent:	Thank you for your time, Mr./Mrs./Ms. _____.
Teacher:	I'm glad I could help you. Thank you for coming. And if you ever have any other problems, please call me again. Goodbye.

VI. Asking for More Information:

Work with a group of three to five students. Write down five problems that an elementary school student might have. Then write down the advice that a teacher and/or parents can give to help solve the problem.

Problem #1: _____
Advice: _____
Problem #2: _____
Advice: _____
Problem #3: _____
Advice: _____
Problem #4: _____
Advice: _____
Problem #5: _____
Advice: _____

VII. Grammar Check:

"Make" and **"Let"**: We use **"make"** when someone of authority (parent, boss, teacher, etc.) tells us that we must do something—even if we don't want to! We use **"let"** when someone allows or gives us permission to do something that we want to do. Look at these examples.

Example:

My mother **makes** me clean my room every weekend.
My parents **let** me borrow their car when they aren't using it.

Now, fill in the blank in each sentence below with the correct grammatical form of **"make"** or **"let."**

1. The police _____ me pay a fine of ¥7,000 when I didn't stop on the stopping line.
2. My friend _____ me use his mechanical pencil.
3. Did you _____ your little brother use your computer? I think he broke it.
4. Mr. Wilson _____ Takumi do his homework again because he made so many mistakes.
5. His boss always _____ him have the extra box lunch to take home.
6. My mother _____ me drive her to the station when it rains even when I am very busy.
7. Don't ever _____ Sally use your cell phone. She used mine, and the next month, I had to pay a lot.
8. I can't believe our teacher _____ us go home early today. Last week he _____ us stay 15 minutes past the bell.

Unit 12 Bullying and Other Problems 111

VIII. Look At This:

Look at this list of situations that exist at some schools in Japan. Put an X by those you have seen or heard about. Then add two other situations that you can think of. Finally, get together in a group and ask one another questions about where you have seen the situation, how it was dealt with, and so on.

Absenteeism ☐
Truancy ☐
School refusal ☐
Bullying ☐
Returnees ☐   (students returning to Japan after living overseas for a long time)
Hikikomori ☐
Suicide ☐
Domestic Violence ☐
_____ ☐
_____ ☐

IX. Conversation Practice:

Work with a partner. Use what you have learned in this unit to make a conversation about a problem in an elementary school. Then practice the conversation with your partner, once as Student A and then again as Student B.

Student A: _____

Student B: _____

Student A: _____

Student B: _____

Student A: _____

Student B: _____

Student A: _____

Student B: _____

Student A: _____

Student B: _____

Student A: _____

Student B: _____

Review   Units 9 – 12

I. Unit 9: Physical Education and Health

A. Write complete questions based on the hints below. Use the correct form of **"do," "go,"** or **"play"** as needed.

1. (What sports, you, junior high school?)

   _____

2. (you, hiking, last weekend?)

   _____

3. (How often, he, karate?)

   _____

4. (you, jogging, every day?)

   _____

5. (your brother, basketball?)

   _____

6. (you, yoga, every morning?)

   _____

7. (she, swimming, yesterday?)

   _____

8. (they, track and field, every afternoon?)

   _____

B. Now work with a partner. Take turns asking and answering questions about the sports and clubs you took part in at junior high and high school. Write your and his/her answers on the lines below. See p.86 for reference.

You: (junior high school) _____

  (high school) _____

Your Partner: (junior high school) _____

  (high school) _____

C. Fill in the blank in each sentence below with the correct form of a word or phrase in this box.

> two left feet   head start   break up   compulsory   license   hip-hop
> P.E. (Physical Education)   female   martial arts   What's up

1. I need to get an international driving _____ so that I can drive during my trip to the United States.

2. My sister really loves practicing _____ dance at her junior high school.

3. It is _____ for Japanese children to attend elementary and junior high school.

4. I didn't like _____ class at school because I am bad at sports.

5. Whenever I call my friend on the phone, she answers by asking, "_____?"

6. My son loves _____. His favorites are karate and judo.

7. My best friend is sad because she _____ with her boyfriend last week.

8. I got up early this morning because I wanted to get a _____ on my housework.

9. When I try to dance, it seems as if I have _____!

10. In our junior high school class, we had more male students than _____ students.

II. **Unit 10: Nursery School and Day Care**

A. Write complete questions based on the hints. Work with a partner.

1. (you, work?)

2. (you, enjoy, helping out?)

3. (you, volunteer work?)

4. (how many, children, one class?)

5. (how, children, come to school?)

6. (the children, packed lunch?)

7. (the children, enjoy singing?)

8. (you, teach, read and write?)

B. Imagine you are working or volunteering at a nursery school or day-care center. With a partner, take turns asking each other the questions you made on page 115. Write your partner's answers on the lines below.

1. _____
2. _____
3. _____
4. _____
5. _____
6. _____
7. _____
8. _____

C. Fill in the blank in each sentence below with the correct form of a word or phrase in this box.

> has to / doesn't have to   have to / don't have to

1. We _____ get up early to catch the six o'clock bus.
2. Erika _____ teach the children to read and write.
3. _____ your father _____ take the train every day?
4. John has a lot of money, so he _____ worry about paying his school fees.
5. I _____ finish this report by tomorrow.
6. Sunday is a holiday, so we _____ get up early.

Now write two sentences each about something you "have to" or "don't have to" do.

7. _____
8. _____
9. _____
10. _____

III. Unit 11: Educating and Caring

A. Write complete questions based on the hints below. Then write the answers to the questions. Follow this example.

Example: (difficult, your mother, speak English — Yes)
Is it difficult for your mother to speak English?
Yes, it is. She never has a chance to practice.

1. (easy, you, play tennis — No)

2. (difficult, Sue, feed herself — Yes)

3. (easy, Tom, ski — Yes)

4. (difficult, your friend, cook French food — No)

5. (easy, Jane, teach English — Yes)

6. (difficult, Erika, design a website — No)

7. (easy, your uncle, build houses — Yes)

   _____

   _____

8. (difficult, you, finish, homework — Yes)

   _____

   _____

B. Write sentences describing two things that are easy for you to do and two things that are difficult.

Easy: 1. _____
           2. _____

Difficult: 1. _____
           2. _____

C. Fill the blank in each sentence below with the correct form of one of the words or phrases in this box.

> eating utensil   sign language   toiletry kit   diaper
> wheelchair   change of clothes   medication   Braille

1. Tara is packing a _____ for her overnight trip to Mt. Fuji.

2. Because my mother is deaf, I learned _____ when I was a child.

3. I forgot to bring a _____ so I had to buy soap and a toothbrush.

4. Most restaurants have a ramp for easy access by people in _____.

5. The writing system called _____, which is used by blind people, was created by a Frenchman called Louis Braille.

6. _____ are not just for babies; sometimes older children and elderly people need them, too.

7. Before we went camping last week, we bought a new set of _____.

8. She has been taking _____ for her depression for two years.

IV. Unit 12: Bullying and Other Problems

A. Fill in the blank in each sentence below with the correct form of **"let"** or **"make."**

1. The teacher _____ the students have a long recess today.
2. The nurse _____ the patient lie down so that she could take a blood sample.
3. The principal _____ Jack sit in a chair until he could calm down.
4. I _____ my daughter stay out late because she had a party.
5. My boyfriend just got a new sports car, but he won't _____ me drive it!
6. I'm late because my roommate _____ me stop at a convenience store on our way to school.
7. My mother _____ me do the dishes before I left to meet one of my friends.
8. The store clerk _____ Maxine return the blouse because she didn't like the color.

B. Look at the problems below. Discuss each problem with a partner and then write some advice on how to deal with it.

Problem #1: The child is being bullied at school.

_____
_____
_____
_____

Problem #2: The students are very noisy during the lessons.

_____
_____
_____
_____

Problem #3: The student doesn't talk to anyone.

_____
_____
_____
_____

C. Fill in the blank in each sentence below with the correct form of one of the words or phrases in this box.

> attend   put an end to   handle   further   fever
> bully   successful   hurt   quite   slight

1. My son quit going to school because he was being _____ by other students.
2. She couldn't _____ the seminar because she was sick.
3. Ann has so many classes. It is difficult for her to _____ her schedule.
4. Most young people dream of being rich and _____ in the future.
5. My parents made new family rules to _____ my brother being late every night.
6. She was _____ because her boyfriend forgot her birthday.
7. "If there are no _____ questions, let's begin the test."
8. Mr. Suzuki is _____ busy this year because there are so many students in the class.
9. This year, my daughter's grades were only _____ better than last year.
10. I had a _____ and a sore throat, so I went to the doctor.

著作権法上、無断複写・複製は禁じられています。

Student Teacher　　　　　　　　　　　　　　　　　　　　　　　[B-767]
教室で教える人のための『ベーシック コミュニケーション』

1　刷	2014年11月19日	
3　刷	2019年3月28日	
著　者	スーザン・ウィリアムズ	Susan Williams
	ヴィヴィアン・師岡	Vivian Morooka
発行者	南雲　一範	Kazunori Nagumo
発行所	株式会社　南雲堂	
	〒162-0801　東京都新宿区山吹町361	
	NAN'UN-DO Co., Ltd.	
	361 Yamabuki-cho, Shinjuku-ku, Tokyo 162-0801, Japan	
	振替口座：00160-0-46863	
	TEL: 03-3268-2311（代表）／FAX: 03-3269-2486	
編　集	加藤　敦	
製　版	木内　早苗	
装　丁	銀月堂	
検　印	省　略	
コード	ISBN 978-4-523-17767-8　C0082	

Printed in Japan

E-mail　nanundo@post.email.ne.jp
URL　http://www.nanun-do.co.jp/